Kevin Wood

THE BOARD

Kevin Wood

THE BOARD

A chronicle of the decline and fall
of the Pottstown Symphony Orchestra

A study in Ethics and in Mismanagement

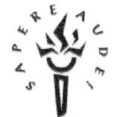

Deutscher Wissenschafts-Verlag (D W V)
Baden-Baden

Umschlaggestaltung: Leonore Wienstrath

Bibliografische Information Der Deutschen Nationalbibliothek
Die Deutsche Nationalbibliothek verzeichnet diese Publikation in der Deutschen Nationalbibliografie; detaillierte bibliografische Daten sind im Internet über http://dnb.ddb.de abrufbar.

Bibliographic information published by Die Deutsche Nationalbibliothek
Die Deutsche Nationalbibliothek lists this publication in the Deutsche Nationalbibliografie; detailed bibliographic data are available in the Internet at http://dnb.ddb.de.

Information bibliographique de Die Deutsche Nationalbibliothek
Die Deutsche Nationalbibliothek a répertorié cette publication dans la Deutsche Nationalbibliografie; les données bibliographiques détaillées peuvent être consultées sur Internet à l'adresse http://dnb.ddb.de.

---

1. Auflage
Gedruckt auf alterungsbeständigem, chlorfrei gebleichtem Papier

© Copyright 2015 by
Deutscher Wissenschafts-Verlag (DWV)®
Postfach 11 01 35
D–76487 Baden-Baden

www.DWV-net.de
www.UniversityPress.de

Alle Rechte, insbesondere das Recht der Vervielfältigung und Verbreitung sowie der Übersetzung, vorbehalten. Kein Teil des Werkes darf in irgendeiner Form (durch Photokopie, Mikrofilm oder ein anderes Verfahren) ohne schriftliche Genehmigung des Verlages reproduziert oder unter Verwendung elektronischer Systeme verarbeitet, vervielfältigt oder verbreitet werden.

ISBN: 978-3-86888-079-3

For
Charles Daniels
Thank you, my friend!

"People remain what they are even if their faces crumble."[1]
Bertolt Brecht

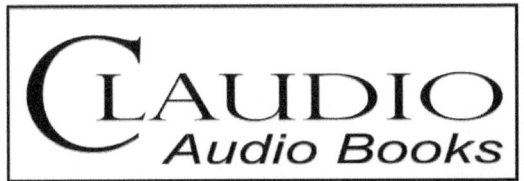

The audio book version of THE BOARD appears on Claudio Records, Catalogue No. CA4729-9, and may be ordered directly at www.claudiorecords.com or from your local bookseller or CD shop.

---

[1] Bertolt Brecht: *In the Jungle of Cities*, Scene 9. Original: *Im Dickicht der Städte*: *"Der Mensch bleibt, was er ist, auch wenn sein Gesicht zerfällt"*. (Suhrkamp Verlag, Berlin, Germany, 1973).

CONTENTS

1. PROLOGUE — 1
2. SUBJECTIVE HISTORY — 7
3. BANKERS, BROKERS, BRAGGARTS & BASTARDS — 32
4. INTERPERSONAL RELATIONSHIPS — 54
5. BOARD MEMBER LOANS — 70
6. MARKETING AND THE PUBLIC — 99
7. ZEBRAS — 116
8. THE LAST YEAR — 129
9. CONCLUSIONS — 143

ACKNOWLEDGMENTS — 153

1. PROLOGUE

In Amsterdam, amid the vitality and tourist throngs in this great city, there exists a magical place. Although prominent on the maps of this metropolis, Vondelpark draws those to it who seek distance. It promises the visitor a moment or a few hours of remoteness from the brutal present or from the merciless past.

Yesterday, sitting alone in this park, Amsterdam's Camelot of the spirit, I began to remember the many, many years and the incidents in life that led me to write this book. What inspired me to begin this narrative was the knowledge, learned on the previous evening, that a dear friend, a brilliant man and one of the greatest musicians of the 20th century will never again be able to share his gifts with the world. The degenerative muscle disease that has befallen him is incurable. I spoke with him yesterday and, afterwards, motivated by the obvious sorrow in his heart; I began to re-trace the years and to catalogue the hurt that so many have lived who have chosen to spend their lives in the arts. Somehow, speaking with him had completed this circle.

It is not to say that this man in Amsterdam has been, directly or even indirectly, a protagonist here or one of the subjects of this book. Others have had that dubious honor. What, however, is intended in this story is to show the fragility of life devoted to music and to do so through one example of how it must not always be. For those who have made this decision to trust their lives to this mechanism of communication, to this language of the spirit, to this pure form of intellect, they soon learn that their livelihoods and those of their families and loved-ones often hang on the thinnest of threads.

We deceive ourselves. We forget, especially in the United States, how the function or dysfunction of the administration of an arts institution can destroy lives, dreams and careers. Naïve as it may be, we forget the role of the boards of directors which govern these institutions, persons with the responsibility of stewardship but amateurs in the increasingly complex constellation of musicians, unions, funders, law, marketing and the public. In our passion to create we allow ourselves to sit back in awe of their collective might and often passively watch the rape of the thing we love best, of the vision to which we have dedicated our lives.

Yesterday, in Vondelpark, across from the film institute, I watched the birds and listened for the captive parrots who have long been the star residents of this green island in the midst of a European capital of art and culture. Sitting there, my thoughts went back to the incidents in the United States, to a place called Pottstown, Pennsylvania, and to a cultural milestone that had been built there but to fall prey to the wrecker's ball of board incompetence and fiscal and social irresponsibility.

As my friend in Amsterdam and his family battle with other circumstances, not in any way related to this story, which have torn him from the midst of life, I think back to others who are and were direct victims of Pottstown's exercise in human disdain. There was the Music Director, a brilliantly talented woman who gave of herself to make of a second-rate orchestra one of which she and the community could be proud. She knew what this would mean to her and to her future and to her husband, himself an accomplished musician, and she made of this orchestra a second self. She became the ensemble, lending extraordinary creativity, financial assistance and patience to the development of an orchestra in which she believed and for which she sacrificed so much. For this reason alone, the deception and the indignation she lived and has continued to live in subsequent years has magnified the hurt and the depth of this loss.

There are or were those musicians who looked proudly upon what was being created here. They have also been deceived. They had given their trust to a board of directors that had not earned that trust. Some have gone on to other endeavors but for others, those who fought to keep this dream alive, the void goes beyond the mere loss of income and of prestige in their community. Their tragedy is to be seen and judged on a much deeper, personal level. These men and women have been emotionally violated. Some, the more intelligent of them, now know and understand what had happened there. They know who, stealthily and with intent, conspired to undo that which would have been, and was beginning to become, the one note of distinction in a forgotten, abandoned, impoverished and drug-ridden community.

My story here as the final chief executive of this institution, is perhaps not so important. In writing this book, however, it is my wish to leave behind a road map for future, young executive directors who may be tempted to risk their talents, vision and livelihoods and show their willingness to take the rudder of such an organization as I did in Pottstown. To these young persons, eager to prove their worth and climb the ladder to success within other, established institutions, this story hopes to make you aware of the many red flags and sometimes insurmountable hurdles that you will certainly confront and that will challenge your sense of justice and self-worth. This book is about such things but also about subjective history, employer responsibility and irresponsibility and, above all, about greed. This book hopes to tell the tale of how a body of unknowing amateurs first engaged experienced professionals to steer their orchestra then usurped the authority given to these professionals and, finally, sabotaged all they had accomplished for the institution and for the community, itself. As with many such ensembles, this board saw itself as more important than the orchestra. In this posturing, they forgot the tale of the "Emperor's New Clothes". Years later, after the music director, the chief executive, many musicians, key and influential board members, funders and others had abandoned them, did they finally begin to become aware of their nakedness.

It was, at that point in this devolutionary tale, too late for the community. It was, however, also too late for those who chose to leave this chapter in human arrogance to a hopefully soon-to-be-forgotten past and to risk a new start in a treacherous and unforgiving profession. It was too late for the conductor who, despite talent and creativity and a will to go on, struggles yet with the consequences of her morally correct and personally difficult decision to leave this board and these people and this experience to her past.

It is too late for me and for the personal and financial consequences these years have brought with them and it is too late for my partner there who, with a progressive eye disease and a stroke behind her, is sure that both were exacerbated by the pressures under which I had to live and work, pressures that had damaged my health as well.

However, dear reader, my intent in this book is neither to preach nor to awaken any sense of pity or other feelings for or against those in this story. I tell you these things because, as we all too readily forget, career decisions always bring with them personal developments, be they good or bad. Because living is also an art form, a painting or as many believe, an unwritten novel, these subtle shadows are not to be ignored.

My thoughts return me to that park in which this narrative began. These thoughts remind me of the greatness in every honest and selfless human being, of greatness and potential that can thrive given the right balances in life. This equation brings with it a measure of love, a drop or two of creativity and energy and, above all, a large amount of social responsibility. It is this last ingredient so sorely missing in this tale and which wrecked this vessel on the rocks of inhuman behavior and unthinking selfishness.

With these thoughts I left Vondelpark on that afternoon, thinking of the masses of hurt that go into making art. I thought, too, how important art is for humankind and how thoughtlessly this same humankind can destroy that which makes the spirit so unique among creatures in this universe.

This story of the rise and fall of the Pottstown Symphony Orchestra is more than just the chronology of mismanagement of an organization at the board level in the United States. The systems used to govern arts institutions, worldwide, each vary in ways where such unthinking and self-serving policies as I describe in this book – be they in the context of a board or of another, strictly European administrative structure – can put the organization itself and its survival at risk.

The issues presented here are international ones. They are also issues of local importance. It makes no difference whether the organizational structure of a cultural institution is based on the German/Austrian "Intendant" model, on the US/UK/Canadian establishment of boards of directors or on a hybrid governance structure which, more or less, derives its authority from either its relationships to governmental support or to private funding or, as is the case here, from its presumed primacy as an integral societal network. Regardless of the structure, the potential for corruption is not and can never be completely eliminated. This potential reaches the stage of an administrative melt-down when those in power forget, or chose to ignore, the rationale behind their position in the organization. This melt-down becomes reality when the "me" element begins to supersede the sense of "we" or "us". As in any dictatorship, the implosion is slow in coming but is, nevertheless, inevitable. That is what happened in Pottstown.

The irrational fear of the board of directors of the Pottstown Symphony Orchestra Association that it would cease to become important as a *prima facie* social entity if the orchestra were to achieve regional and broader importance, plus the board's fear of fundraising, led to irrational pronouncements, abuse of employees and a hatred directed at those who sought to effect change and administrative, artistic and financial stability. The despotic elements in this organization went so far as to impeach a fellow board member, one who was also an active fundraiser and tireless advocate for the organization, because he expressed his anger at the stubbornness and the rigidity the board as a whole had assumed, defending itself against the increasing need to care for the organization's financial health. Thereafter, the internal decay progressed quickly. Within a year, the Pottstown Symphony was on life support. As a musical institution, as a body of persons, it was terminally ill. However, forever in denial, it was to be another two years before the slow removal of its life-support systems, coupled with a level of debt that never disappeared, continued refusal to engage in genuine development campaigns and a deep-rooted denial psychosis, brought the organization to its long-awaited end. At its death, the Pottstown Symphony was still in its youth, in a period that should have promised great things for such an ensemble. It died of its addiction to its own importance and of a potent social drug known as greed and power.

This is the story of an organization that had lost itself or, perhaps, had not really known itself from the beginning. This is a parable of success turned into failure by those for whom success was a threat to their sense of self-importance. It is also the story of undemocratic processes at work and of an incestuous style of governance that chose to deny the advice and direction of professionals, both employees and those at the board level, engaged to make of the Pottstown Symphony an important regional orchestra. Instead of welcoming the attention their ensemble was starting to enjoy, they conspired among themselves to annul the influence of those very persons engaged to fulfill this mission and who had been successful in doing so. As professionals in the thankless business of arts and orchestra management, we are employed at the service of boards of directors compiled or recruited from politics, education, business and the community. This circumstance requires of us a certain but high degree of professionalism, persuasive ability and diplomacy. It is also our mandate to educate those sitting on our boards about the complexities of our and their institution, the interplay of marketing, finance and art and their role as provider and care-giver for the organization. When those entrusted with this care-giver role refuse to accept that with the visibility in their community and with the authority that comes with a seat on the symphony or arts board there also comes a moral and fiscal responsibility and when those members refuse to acknowledge that responsibility and act accordingly to protect their institution from bankruptcy and loss of status, there then exists a condition one can only describe as corrupt. There is passive corruption and active corruption. Passive corruption exists when there has been no warning of the danger to come and the organization sinks into oblivion without board members or staff recognizing the warnings and acting on them. Corruption becomes active when the warnings have been given, the consequences of non-action been made clear and the situation critical. It becomes active when, despite all these things the board and its members see themselves as more important than the institution itself, more valuable than their employees and more significant than the organization's value to their community. This is what happened in Pottstown and this is the story of an organization that did not need to die but for which there was no reprieve. The Pottstown Symphony was the victim of this same active corruption.

In the chapters to come, I will attempt to highlight and reflect on the individual circumstances, influences at play on many levels of the orchestral administration and its board that led to its fall. This book is for you who are starting out in this business as well as for those who wish to prevent a similar fate from befalling their orchestra or arts organization. My hope is that it highlights the warning signs that lead to such behavior and gives you the tools you need to stop the death march and initiate the changes that must occur if such an institution is to survive.

Cicero wrote: "*Quousque tandem abuerte patentia nostra?*"[2] This very abuse of the patience of a community, of those few patrons loyal to this artistic institution and the loyalty of its hard-working employees and of the few arts professionals on its board as well as of others who worked towards ethical and responsible management, were tested on many levels. It is here, in this story of the Pottstown Symphony Orchestra, that so many of these elements come together, all displaying an abuse of trust and uniting in a constellation of incompetence, power and in the context of a diseased global society, that makes this story a cautionary tale.

---

[2] Marcus Tullius Cicero: "How long will you abuse our patience?" *In Catilinam,* I, I, 1

2. SUBJECTIVE HISTORY

Be it a country, an individual or an organization, the version it tells of its history betrays the moral substance which drives and motivates him or it. The airline, Lufthansa, for example, was reorganized at the aegis of the Allied powers following World War II. In essence, the company was "de-Nazified" by the victors although it had played an important role in the war and existed during the Hitler era thanks to the impressed labor of thousands of imprisoned minorities. The role of Lufthansa has slowly begun to enter our understanding of pre and post war history. The official company narrative told of an airline that began and prospered after the war. Even though several Lufthansa facilities around the world have streets and alleys named after pre-war or impressed and imprisoned laborers, many of them also Jews, the company mentions little or nothing of this dark chapter in its history and many of those impressed during the Nazi era, men and women whose lives were broken by the conditions under which they were tied to this yoke of slavery, have seen no reparations, received no apologies or punitive compensation and no acknowledgement of their suffering. On this topic, the website, "Funding Universe" provides an interesting perspective while also admitting that all major German companies during the NSDAP[3] regime were also organs of and under control of the Nazi dictator. "Regarded as an instrument of the state, Lufthansa increasingly came under the control of the ruling Nazi Party. Lufthansa began service to destinations in the Soviet Union during 1940. These routes provided the German Luftwaffe ("air force") with valuable strategic information used in Hitler's surprise invasion of the Soviet Union two years later."[4] More to the point, however, is an article which appeared in the German magazine, Focus, which reported in 2010 on a documentary film produced by the French-German TV Station, ARTE, about Lufthansa and its role as Nazi collaborator before and during World War II. In a report issued by the Deutsche Presse Agentur, Focus reported: "To the history of the airline belongs the fact that, in 1933, immediately following the NAZI assumption of power and behind the mask of civil aviation, the preparation for a completely new dimension in aggressive warfare had begun. The strict regulations of the Treaty of Versailles had forbidden the German Reich to form an air force. For this reason, Germany's dictator, Adolf Hitler, came to an agreement with the directors of Lufthansa. Behind the curtain of peaceful usage, passenger

---

[3] Nationalsozialistische Deutsche Arbeiterpartei or Nazi Party.
[4] http://www.fundinguniverse.com/company-histories/Deutsche-Lufthansa-AG-company-History.html.

planes should be produced which at a later time and with simple means could be retooled to accommodate bombs. The new machines were made available to the Lufthansa which used them to train its pilots. And Hitler's planning assigned still a further role to Lufthansa. The airline was to take over the maintenance and repair of airplanes behind the front lines. For this, in the conquered and occupied lands, local laborers were recruited and in increasing numbers they started using impressed and slave labor."[5]

However, Lufthansa goes on and has become one of the great personnel and freight carriers of post-war Europe. Such an organization can, thanks to its size and to its wealth, hide the shadowy past it wishes to forget and, de facto, has forgotten. From time to time someone casts a bit of light into this darkness but, for the most part, no one really cares any more. It all happened so very long ago and, soon, there will be no more survivors and the records, locked in safes in company headquarters around the globe, will never again really see the light of day. They will never be substantially analyzed by historians or by governments. The wealth the company has at its disposal is a powerful defense against this analysis and against the prying eyes of scholars, researchers of all kinds and against an ever-curious justice system.

The same is true for the US corporate giant, IBM. This American conglomerate's development and sale of its punched-card technology to the Nazis for the administration of the concentration camps before the war and the further development of the system and sale of improved versions of this early computerization to Germany after December 7th 1941, is a scandal that has never genuinely been explored. The fact that the executives at IBM were never called to task during the Nuremberg trials is a further document to the use of history as a means of subjective cleansing.[6] In his book, "IBM and the Holocaust", Edwin Black writes: "Most of the national socialist concentration camps had available to them a so-called Hollerith Department. In certain KZs[7] such as, for example, Dachau and Storkow, IBM had installed up to two dozen sorting machines, tabulation machines and printers.[8] Other camps possessed punching machines and transferred the cards from there to the central bureaus such as Mauthausen or Berlin.[9]...Because every step in the life of a prisoner was regulated and

---

[5] http://www.focus.de/kultur/kino_tv/medien-arte-doku-ueber-die-lufthansa-in-der-ns-zeit_aid_532708.html?drucken=1.
[6] Edwin Black: *IBM and the Holocaust*. Crown Publishing Group, New York, 2001.
[7] Konzentrationslager or Concentration Camp.
[8] Secret XL 8486, PW Intelligence Bulletin No. 2/57, 25 April 1945.
[9] Letter from Kommandantur Arbeitseinsatz Mauthausen to Arbeitseinsatz Ravensbrück from 27 November 1944.

recorded, a regular exchange of lists, punched cards and coded documents was made necessary."[10]

But what of the history of smaller companies, of persons of less wealth and influence or of an organization which carries a public mandate? For these, there are other rules and expectations. Especially for cultural institutions, the degree of objectivity in their historical narrative betrays the credibility of the organization itself. The ability, in a moral sense, and willingness to look back and evaluate one's own past in and with a healthy degree of objectivity, also tells of the ability of the group or organization in question to confront and deal with the existential realities it must face.

The history of the symphony orchestra in Pottstown is one of an organization which had fallen victim to this subjective correction of its own past. On its web site and in its literature, as well as in countless internal documents and during board of directors' and other meetings and conferences held under the organization's auspices, the history of the Pottstown Symphony was told as if it were a saga of the heroic act and brilliant idea coming from a single man who, following his death, passed the torch on to the next and subsequent generations. It was Pottstown's "Tain" or "Nibelungenlied" or its own and unique version of "Paul Bunyan". The local Pottstown newspaper, The Mercury, summarized this heroic tale in an article it published in February, 1991. The reporter, Andrea Kerr, wrote the following: "Now 35 years have passed since area resident and conductor William F. Lamb realized his dream to bring a symphony orchestra to his hometown. In the spring of 1964, 800 people gathered to hear Lamb and other local musicians perform an inaugural concert at Pottstown High School. Lamb's dream was such a success that the orchestra is still entertaining music lovers today."[11]

Until the orchestra's demise, presumably sometime in late 2010 or early 2011, this story was and remained the official narrative. Without reservation, this is a wonderful tale. It speaks of the heroic vision of one man who sacrificed all to bring culture to the area and to realize his lifelong dream of standing at the head of an orchestra of his own creation. If taken at face value, there can be no objection to or criticism of this sterling example of American integrity and independent thinking.

Had the symphony not collapsed under the weight of its ponderous mismanagement, this tale would have been told and retold for decades to

---

[10] Edwin Black: *IBM and the Holocaust*. Crown Publishing Group, New York, 2001. Translated from the German by this author.

[11] Andrea Kerr: "In Pottstown There's Something for Everyone". The Pottstown Mercury. 28 February 1991.

come. That is, if the weight of economic and moral decay had not had its effect on the orchestra's future or lack of one.

In any event, the official story told within the Pottstown Symphony seemed to me to be, increasingly, a means of perpetuating the myth which drove the board's loyalty to the status quo it had created for itself. In particular, the presence of the daughter of the lauded hero and official founder of the Pottstown Symphony on its board and her stubborn insistence that she be recognized as such and that the wishes of her father, as she understood them, were to become the catechism under which the symphony was to operate in perpetuity, became an inviolable principle under which the organization was governed. It was in the best interests of the members of the board of directors to perpetuate this tale. These members of the board, led by a former school teacher and former superintendent of schools, lived and breathed with and gained public acknowledgement from this blood line. This acknowledgement also made them presume to be powerful and influential, a presumption that their increasing debt, failed management style and refusal to fundraise, and the global market crash of 2008 quickly laid to rest.

After the dust had settled, ancient facts began to appear which cast the shadow of doubt on the bright and heroic tale of Mr. Lamb and his dream. Among other documents, there appeared the following passage in a "History of Pottstown", published in 1953 by the Pottstown Historical Society and to which I was allowed access thanks to the curator of this archive. In this highly interesting story of the town's history, there appears one paragraph which seems to tell a different if less heroic tale of the first days of the Pottstown Symphony Orchestra.

"It had only been recently that Pottstown has had wider opportunities in music. Successful choral groups, like the Meistersingers and the Melody Maids have been formed. For a number of years the Pottstown Symphony Orchestra has continually rehearsed and given concerts, its conductor, Mr. Kenneth Morse, persisting in spite of numerous handicaps."[12]

Where was Mr. Lamb in 1953 and in the years prior to the publication of this book? How could an orchestra that gave its first concert in the "spring of 1964" have "rehearsed and given concerts" in 1953 and earlier? Why did Mr. Morse disappear from the official history of the Pottstown Symphony and for what reason did he vanish from it? Above all, what were these "numerous handicaps" that hindered Mr. Morse in the realization of his vision for this orchestra? Had Mr. Morse also fallen victim to the apathy that, over 50 years

---

[12] P. Chancellor & M. Wendell: *A History of Pottstown Pennsylvania* (Pottstown, PA: Historical Society of Pottstown 1953. PP 177-178).

later, would seal the death of this ensemble? This same source gives us somewhat more insight into these origins. The authors continue: "The most sustained interest seems to have been in a band. A military band played here in 1799, but whether that was a local organization is not known. Later in the century there was Andre's Cornet Band, formed about 1845. It continued for decades until it re-formed as the Pottstown band. In recent years the names of William F. Lamb, Senior and Junior, have been associated with its leadership. The Lambs have also been leaders in music instruction through their long-established studio."[13]

Further research revealed that the origins of the Pottstown Symphony are even older than suggested by Chancellor and Wendell. The symphony seems to have initially been founded by Kenneth Morse in the year 1940. The ensemble, originally called the Pottstown Civic Symphony, enjoyed, initially, a shortened life span haven fallen victim to the national need to do something about Hitler and Mussolini and to the charms of "Rosie the Riveter". Decisive as well was the issue of conscription in the early years of the war and the uncertainties that came with impending military service. The conscription laws in effect at the start of WWII provided for a draft age anywhere between 18 and 65 years old, although seldom were men older than 45 called up for duty. An anomaly is also the provision in that law that made the drafting of women possible in times of war. Although there doesn't seem to have been any instances of women being called into service, the eventuality was provided for. It is also important to note that, in 1940, the life expectancy of males was 63.1 years and of females 66.8, which, with the issue of conscription, the genuine danger of being injured or killed in action in a foreign theatre, and the need to support a family, afforded little reserve time for such activities as an amateur orchestra. The <u>Pottstown Mercury</u> reports, however, a revitalization of the orchestra following the war. "Laudable is the decision of the Pottstown Recreation Commission to sponsor a local civic symphony orchestra. Such sponsorship will mean much to the cultural advancement of the community. Kenneth Morse, a Pottstown accountant, formed a Pottstown Symphony Orchestra before World War II. With the aid of some of his friends of nearby cities, he presented a fine musical organization to Pottstown audiences. Unfortunately, the war came on and interest in Mr. Morse's project lagged…We are glad to see Frances Donnon of the Recreation Commission taking up this fine work. Too often, people think of recreation as only playground work. There's a great deal of recreation in music as well as other hobbies that may be enjoyed by adults"[14]

---

[13] Ibid.
[14] "The Orchestra Revived". Pottstown Mercury and The Pottstown News, 18 November 1948.

According to the account in the Pottstown Mercury, Mr. Morse also seems to have been highly respected in the area: "He is an accomplished director, a fine inspiration to amateur musicians."[15] It is evident from subsequent articles in the years following 1948, that this, second attempt at founding a Pottstown Symphony, proved to be successful. The Pottstown Mercury from 16 November 1953 briefly notes continuing rehearsals of this orchestra, still under the baton of Kenneth Morse: "The Pottstown Civic Symphony Orchestra will hold a rehearsal tonight at 8 o'clock at the Moose auditorium."[16] Evidently not only the support of the Pottstown Recreation Commission but also that of the then existing Moose Lodge contributed substantially to the survival of the Pottstown Symphony. In 1953, The Mercury reported the following: "Kenneth Morse, director of the Pottstown Civic Symphony Orchestra of the Moose lodge, last night announced that rehearsals would be held during summer months. Morse said the purpose of the summer rehearsals is to hold practice for new members wishing to become familiar with symphonic work to obtain experience necessary to join the orchestra in the Fall...'The Lodge is co-operating with the orchestra', Morse said, 'so that Pottstown may have a recognized symphony in the community.'"[17]

In the chronology of the Pottstown Symphony during its early years, the initial support of the Pottstown Recreation Commission seems to have disappeared sometime in the early or mid-1950's. Again, The Mercury reports on the support the symphony received which seems at this point to have come entirely from the Moose Lodge. "The 7:45 p.m. rehearsal at the Moose auditorium will include Schubert's sixth and Beethoven's fifth symphonies...John Atkinson and Albert Piazza are on the Moose music committee. The local lodge sponsors the symphony project."[18]

It is my belief that the probable rationale behind this decision to selectively retell the history of the Pottstown Symphony and to relegate Mr. Morse to eternal anonymity was a commercial one. It is known that Mr. Lamb was a highly esteemed, professional musician in the region. He played trumpet in the Pottstown Town Band and, until 1963, was also its music director. He is reported to have also played in the fledgling Pottstown Symphony. At the start of World War II, Lamb became the solo trumpeter for the United States Military Band in Washington, DC and continued to perform with the band until the end of the war, in 1945. Sometime after late 1946 or early 1947, he

---

[15] Ibid.
[16] Pottstown Mercury from 16 November 1953.
[17] Pottstown Mercury from 26 May 1953.
[18] Pottstown Mercury from 07 December 1953.

was also the owner of Lamb's Music House in Pottstown, a business he inherited from his father, W.F. Lamb who retired in January 1947[19]. With relative certainty, one can surmise that Lamb's Music House profited from the sale of sheet music and of instruments, from replacement parts for instruments and from repairs and from the giving of music lessons there. This is normal for such an establishment and the retail music business functions very much the same today as it did in 1953 or 1964. The <u>Pottstown Mercury</u> in its article on Mr. Lamb's retirement, points out that Mr. Lamb was regarded as a "civic leader,"[20] a factor which the available facts lead this author to conclude that he may have also had an influence on the Recreation Commission in its early decision to support the founding of a Pottstown Symphony in 1940 and 1948. It is also interesting to note, however, that there are no further records to be found which tell of the development and/or of the fate of the Pottstown Symphony in the years following 1953 and until 1963 or 1964. An attempt to research these records was defeated by the inordinate and misplaced loyalty of a hired researcher to the preservation of the status quo in Pottstown. Upon learning of the nature of this book, she withdrew from the project entirely, refusing to further assist this author in the search for the genuine origins of the Pottstown Symphony. Also, no obituary for Mr. Morse has been found although 1940 census records for an accountant (bookkeeper per the census document) by the same name and living in Pottstown at the time indicate that he was born in 1910 on Long Island, in Nassau County, New York. Further research, however, shows that he had died in Portland, Maine in 1983 at the age of 73. There is also suggestion of a connection with the New England Music Camp in the vicinity of Portland which was supported by a patron of the Pottstown Symphony who later would protest against any thought of a name-change for the orchestra and who, probably, would also have known Mr. Morse both in Pottstown as well as in Maine since, as you will recall, Morse spent his final years in that state and the above mentioned associate had been affiliated with the camp since 1981. At the time he founded the Pottstown Symphony, Kenneth Morse was 30 years old. He was the sole Kenneth Morse in the community and the sole accountant in Pottstown with the family name Morse so it is highly unlikely that he could have been confused with another Morse living in Pottstown at this time. He was also an associate of Raymond Elliott, the president of the then 1st Federal Bank, later known as the Susquehanna Savings and Loan, who was an accomplished violinist. It was Elliott who, reportedly, also played in the Pottstown Symphony under Morse and who, during his time in the military, performed along with Virgil Fox at

---

[19] Pottstown Mercury from 18 January 1947, page 1.
[20] Ibid.

Ft. Dix in New Jersey. In 1953, the Pottstown Mercury makes mention of an Elliott String Ensemble and of its performance in concert at the Grace Lutheran Church in Royersford, PA.[21] This attests to, at least, a hint of professional activity by Mr. Elliott outside of his role as an accountant and bank president. Interestingly, Morse and Elliott were both accountants and both would have had a professional association which expanded to also encompass their musical cooperation under the umbrella of the Pottstown Symphony. Unfortunately, the Pottstown Mercury article doesn't see fit to mention the names of the individual musicians however, knowing of the association it is highly likely that the contrabass player in the Elliott String Ensemble was, most probably, Kenneth Morse.

This revised story of the creation of the Pottstown Symphony is further supported by empirical evidence supplied by the United States Census. Every 10 years, the US Government engages in a count of its citizens which also includes their professional designations, ages and data on the demographics of the communities in which people live. When applied to the years between 1940 and 1960, the period between the founding of the Pottstown Symphony by Mr. Morse and the presumed re-founding by William Lamb, the statistics point directly to a probable association between the two. In 1940, the population of the USA was 123,164,569. This population increased by close to 30 million persons in 1950 and by another 28 million in 1960 for a total population in 1960 of 179,323,175[22]. Parallel to this, the core community in Pottstown increased by an average of 3,000 persons in each of these 10 year periods, with this population reaching a peak in 1960 of 26,144[23]. Statistically, the US Government reported approximately 160,000 persons in the USA in each of the census reports of 1940, 1950 and 1960, persons who indicated their profession as either professional musician or as a composer[24]. On the average, this would mean that 0.12% of the US population consisted of professional musicians, a figure which, when extended to the Pottstown population, would mean that there were an average of between 24 and 31 professional musicians in Pottstown in each of the census periods ending in 1940, 1950 and 1960. However, this figure does not take into account those who would have only expressed interest in pop music or those who simply called themselves "professionals" without the ability to actively engage in a career as a working musician. Also, the statistically small numbers of persons interested in classical music would have reduced this figure substantially so

---

[21] "Lutheran Church to Hear Ensemble Palm Sunday" Pottstown Mercury, 16 March 1953.
[22] http://en.wikipedia.org/wiki/United_States_Census.
[23] http://en.wikipedia.org/wiki/Pottstown,_Pennsylvania.
[24] http://answers.google.com/answers/threadview?id=127434.

that this author surmises that there would have been no more than between 15 and 20 classically trained musicians in Pottstown who also were technically capable of performing in a symphony orchestra and would or could have shown the interest in doing so. It is hardly thinkable that these musicians, this small number of between 15 and 20 professionals, would also not have known one another, would not have performed together and, in Pottstown, would not have all congregated in and around Lamb's Music Shop. This fact casts a light on the dubious reporting by <u>The Mercury</u> in an article published on 23 October 1963: "Former musicians and persons with a passion for music have a chance to become part of the first Pottstown orchestra, which is being organized by William F. Lamb Jr., former director of the famed Pottstown Band."[25] If we assume that Kenneth Morse's orchestra would have existed past December 1953, and there is no reason to conclude that it did not, the gap between the end of that ensemble's history and the beginning of that for Mr. Lamb's ensemble would not have been more than a few years.

It is my presumption that at some time around 1960, if not shortly before, the Pottstown Civic Symphony under Kenneth Morse had, for whatever reasons, probably financial, simply ceased to function. It was in 1962 or 1963 that the first murmurs regarding a Pottstown Symphony under William Lamb began to be heard. The methodology of his recruitment of players for this resurrected orchestra was very similar to that of Mr. Morse. This methodology was, simply, to recruit his musicians from outside the region, something Morse had done repeatedly and with great success. This same article in <u>The Mercury</u> from 23 October 1963 documents this as follows: "Lamb noted that the invitation to become a member of the first Pottstown Orchestra extends not only to the immediate Pottstown area, but to those persons living in Boyertown, Northern Chester County, Spring City, Royersford, Birdsboro and other areas."[26] Also conspicuous in this report is the undeniable fact that this Pottstown orchestra was anything but a "professional" one. The call for players went out as follows: "Are you an out-of-towner who played violin in high school but since have played little? Does your musical taste hunger for participation in the big sound of an orchestra?"[27] This is hardly the appeal for a fully-professional orchestra and echoes the same arguments made by Mr. Morse just a few years before: "Morse said the purpose of the summer rehearsals is to hold practice for new

---

[25] "String Musicians Needed for Pottstown Orchestra". Pottstown Mercury from 23 October 1963.
[26] Ibid.
[27] Ibid.

members wishing to become familiar with symphonic work to obtain experience necessary to join the orchestra in the fall."[28]

At the risk of being accused of an over-prejudicial evaluation of these facts, I must come to the irreversible conclusion that either influential persons associated with the symphony board or, indeed, Mr. Lamb and his family, thought it best to ban Mr. Morse to the purgatory of anonymity and to re-tell the symphony's creation story, this time in their private and very unique image and likeness. This makes good business sense so long as the music store remained open. After it closed its doors, this tale became a means to an end and added to Mr. Lamb's credibility within the Pottstown School system where he had become head of music. The telling and re-telling of this version of history later made of the power brokers on the Pottstown Symphony's board of directors, together with the surviving daughter of the presumed and much lauded, creative founder of the symphony a work of historical continuity in the eyes of the Pottstown folk who, conveniently, forgot that Mr. Morse had ever lived.

From sources who had been in Pottstown during this time I learned that the symphony had actually been founded on the basis of the Pottstown Town Band which further binds the work of Kenneth Morse to that of William Lamb since the Lambs, father and son, were active with the band before and after the tenure of Mr. Morse in Pottstown. The Moose Lodge as venue for this founding gesture has been documented as well as the fact that the Moose Lodge also possessed a significant library of orchestral music which it put at the disposal of the Pottstown Symphony during these early years. However, there is also a historical church in the village, Emmanuel Lutheran, that has a place on the National Register of Historic Places and which figures significantly into this history. In fact, in a closet at Emmanuel Lutheran one could, until recently, find an old contrabass, very much in disrepair, that was one of the first instruments in the possession of the newly founded Pottstown Symphony and which presumably had belonged to or been used by Mr. Morse, as well as a large music library consisting of orchestral scores and parts with repertoire that matches the programming Mr. Morse selected for his fledgling ensemble. Unfortunately, in a wave of housecleaning in the church in 2009, this substantial orchestral library was discarded.

In the years subsequent to 1953, the Pottstown Symphony as well as the Pottstown Town Band rehearsed at Emmanuel Lutheran Church and, later, also at Christ Episcopal Church in Pottstown. Although Emmanuel Lutheran maintains that there was no connection between the symphony and the church, the former Organist and Director of Music at Emmanuel,

---

[28] Pottstown Mercury from 26 May 1953.

Dr. William Nash, tells a different story. A number of years ago, with the assistance of a researcher, Ruth Neeb, who died in late 2011 or early 2012, Nash undertook a study of the musical life at Emmanuel from the beginnings of the congregation almost two centuries ago. While employed at Emmanuel as its organist and music director, he published a pamphlet which told the story of the organ and of the Tiffany stained glass windows in the main chapel and was preparing to release a second volume detailing the rest of the church's musical history which would have also included the involvement of the Pottstown Symphony and of the Pottstown Town Band in the church using it as a rehearsal venue. The housecleaning which led to the destruction of the music library in 2009 was carried out during a time when Dr. Nash was recovering from an illness. He learned of this action much too late to have stopped it, being informed by the janitor at a later time. The loss of this material, all of which probably belonged to either the symphony or to the successor to the Moose Lodge, later known as the Elks, was a blow to any research into the origins of the orchestra after 1953. In 2009, Dr. Nash ended his employment with Emmanuel Lutheran. Upon doing so, he left behind the research he and his assistant had conducted which may have filled in the gap between the years 1953 and 1964. What was clear from conversations with Dr. Nash is that there was a strong connection between the Pottstown Town Band and the orchestra with William Lamb being part of both organizations. He is thought to have played trumpet in the Pottstown Civic Symphony under Kenneth Morse, at least on a substitute basis, and is known to have conducted the Pottstown Town Band, a position which he resigned in 1963 shortly before his re-founding of the Pottstown orchestra. Also Lamb's Music House played a role in this development since several of the instrumental teachers Lamb had employed with his music business also performed in both the orchestra and in the band. In 2012 this author initiated contact to Emmanuel Lutheran Church in an attempt to further document this association with the congregation. I was informed by them that they had no records detailing any association between the church and the symphony. Thereafter, I further contacted Dr. Nash who requested a colleague associated with the church to obtain access to the already published history of the organ but also to a ring binder containing the notes he and Ruth Neebe had compiled regarding the past musical history of the church. It is reported to this author that around the time of my inquiry into the association between the symphony and Emmanuel, this research material in this binder had been lost or discarded.[29] However, it is not presently and was not historically customary in Pottstown to codify such partnerships by

---

[29] Telephone conversation and oral history report from Dr. William Nash from 11 September 2012.

means of contracts or letters of agreement and it is highly likely that this cooperative enterprise was handled in the same fashion, a handshake sufficing to cement a usage agreement between the church and the Pottstown Symphony.

The association between Kenneth Morse and Raymond Elliott having been established, it remains to also document the association between William Lamb and Mr. Elliott. The Reading Eagle reported on the Pottstown Symphony in an article released in 1964: "There are many men involved. But the leaders are William F. Lamb, Jr., owner of Lamb's Music House and a former solo trumpeter in the U.S. Army Band, and Raymond S. Elliott, a violinist of some accomplishment who happens to be president of Pottstown's First Federal Savings & Loan Association...Elliott says the symphony is budgeted at about $1,800 per concert, with 1,000 patron sales being sufficient for two regular concerts."[30]

What seems to have happened in 1963 or 1964 was the fusion of ideas coming from the Pottstown Civic Symphony which probably had ceased to exist at this time but whose creative energies through the association between Morse and Elliott, among others, were kept alive through the creativity of Raymond Elliott and his Little Orchestra Society, an organization entirely supported by Elliott's bank, and with Mr. Lamb as the catalyst, resulted in a structural entity now known as the Pottstown Symphony. In the same article, the Reading Eagle reports: "In the meantime, the orchestra's sponsoring unit has been set on formal, non-profit lines as the Pottstown Symphony Orchestra Association. The unusual thing about it is that Elliott is president of the board and plays violin in the orchestra."[31] In further researching the origins of the Pottstown Symphony, however, one also comes across an interesting chronology known as "Sheila's Corner", a web site devoted to supporting American symphony orchestras. Under this source, one finds the creation date for the Pottstown Symphony listed as 1954, exactly 10 years prior to the official founding date for the orchestra.[32] It is possible that this date is either in error or that it refers to the Pottstown Civic Symphony but, at very least, it extends the life of that orchestra into a period immediately preceding the presumed founding of the Pottstown Symphony by William Lamb.

However, the commonalities between the later Pottstown Symphony and the Pottstown Civic Symphony under Kenneth Morse do not end with the associations between Morse and Elliott and Lamb and Elliott. Both

---

[30] Reading Eagle. 01 November 1964.
[31] Ibid.
[32] www.sheilascorner.com.

organizations used the same venue for their appearances, albeit decades apart. The Reading Eagle reports as follows: "Otto Wittich, violinist and concertmaster of the Reading Symphony Orchestra, will serve in the same capacity with the Pottstown Civic Symphony Orchestra during the concert at the Pottstown High School auditorium at 2:30 o'clock Saturday afternoon."[33]

The Pottstown Town Band and, in fact, musical ensembles in general, seem to have enjoyed a rich tradition in the area. There is mention of a Mechanics' Band of Pottstown as early as 1843 and of a certain E. Gates who was the then director of that ensemble and, on 27 July 1887, the Montgomery Ledger printed the following: "We have a couple of good bands in Pottstown now, and it is to be hoped they may always be highly appreciated and meet with financial success, though past experience in that respect is not as encouraging as it should be. With all the trouble taken to organize the bands, the long training and skill of the members, and the good music they furnished, their labor in that direction never paid them, either in hard cash, as to health, or in any other way."[34] Even as far back as the late 19th century, there was a general bemoaning of the lack of public support for music in the region with the initial support offered by the Recreation Commission in the 1940's seemingly the only moment of inspiration in a community that has notoriously ignored the effect of the arts on its people and its attractiveness as a place to live: "It cost considerable to buy your uniform and your horn, (to say nothing of "horns" of another kind) and when you left your work at home to attend a band engagement it was almost always at a loss."[35] Of course, as a pleasant pastime, the band culture in Pottstown continued to have its adherents. An obituary for a former Pottstown Band director, Eugene Weidner, appeared in the local newspaper, The Pottstown Mercury, on 09 May 1936. In that obituary it is noteworthy that Mr. Weidner was also "a friend of the late John Philip Sousa. Four years ago (in 1932), he was Sousa's host when the visiting musician was guest conductor for the Ringgold organization. Sousa died the following day and it was Mr. Weidner who arranged for the body's transfer to his home."[36] As the Pottstown Town Band began to lose membership and its musicians became older, others were brought in from outside the region, from Reading and from Philadelphia. The introduction of the local and private string teacher, Theresa Peterson, a violinist who had studied at the Curtis Institute and who could offer Mr. Morse the string players he needed to form an orchestra, completed the

---

[33] Reading Eagle. 27 October 1944.
[34] Montgomery Ledger article from 27 July 1887.
[35] Ibid.
[36] "Eugene Weidner Succumbs To Heart Attack" Pottstown Mercury from 09 May 1936.

picture. As the band disappeared completely in 1991 and with the influx and recruitment of music students from outside the region, as well as the growing emphasis of its music directors on engaging quality players regardless of where they lived, the existence of the Pottstown Symphony was secured. The effective denial of many on the Pottstown Symphony's board of directors in the later years of the orchestra's existence that the musicians in the ensemble came from any place but Pottstown is also refuted in an article in the Pottstown Mercury dated 18 November 1948, which refers to "the aid of some of [Mr. Morse's] friends of nearby cities." In addition, in 1953, the Mercury further reports: "We'll probably have 16 to 20 musicians from Pottstown in the group. The others will come from a surrounding 30-mile area."[37] It has been documented as well that, in 1963, Mr. Lamb expressly stated his wish to recruit from communities far afield of Pottstown. In that article from October 1963 announcing his plans the comparison was made between the re-founded Pottstown Symphony and the legendary Philadelphia Orchestra not 40 miles to the east. The Mercury wrote: "His ambition in providing Pottstown with music of the highest caliber is almost as large as the orchestra he has in mind – 60 to 85 pieces. This is only 25 pieces less than the world-famous Philadelphia Orchestra."[38] From all this it is clear that, even at this early date, the expectation that a competent musical ensemble could be constituted from within Pottstown alone was recognized as an unreasonable and impossible goal.

Aside from this more than substantial body of evidence to support an earlier founding of a symphony in Pottstown, there also exists an interview conducted in 2002 with Mrs. Elsie Huff, a long time Pottstown resident and supporter of the symphony. At the time of this interview, Mrs. Huff would have been 84 years old. Her brief recollection of the tale behind the founding of the Pottstown Symphony is as follows: "The Pottstown Symphony Orchestra was started by my husband and Bill Lamb at our kitchen table while they were discussing ideas for a fledgling Pottstown Band. When Leonard (Huff) was installed as President of Rotary – which met weekly at Brookside Country Club – Bill had the entire band march up the fairway, playing the Battle Hymn of the Republic!"[39] There is an obvious conflict here between the founding story which draws on a rich musical past in Pottstown and that of Mrs. Huff, supported by the Pottstown Symphony board, which talks about a fledgling Pottstown band. However, this discrepancy is to be

---

[37] Pottstown Mercury 23 September 1953, page 5.
[38] "String Musicians Needed for Pottstown Orchestra". The Mercury. 23 October 1963.
[39] Pottstown Historical Society. Oral History. Nancy Dolan: Interview with Elsie Huff, 1918, from February 26, 2002. http://www.pottstownhistory.org.

understood in terms of her husband and Mr. Lamb continuing a legacy or, at least, that is how they and others viewed their role in the history of the Pottstown Symphony. In 1963 or 1964 the Pottstown Band had already existed for quite some time and only gave its last concert sometime in 1991 under the baton of its final music director, Charles Weiser.[40] With the Pottstown Band thriving in 1964, there would have been no reason to found a second such ensemble except, potentially, as competition to the existing one which had been a fixture in Pottstown for over 50 years. In any case, in 1991, when the Pottstown Town Band gave its final concert, Mr. Lamb had already been dead for close to 10 years.

It is known that the Pottstown Town Band, through the activities of the Pottstown Musical Society, was significantly financed by a Mrs. Cory Schumacher. Mrs. Schumacher was also heavily involved in supporting music at Emmanuel Lutheran Church and had brought such legendary artists as Virgil Fox, Jerome Hines and Alexis Weissenberg to Pottstown. However, her activities were not restricted to her role as patron of the arts in that town. She also supported the Reading Musical Foundation which, for years, helped cover the costs for the Reading Pops Orchestra and for the Reading Symphony Orchestra as well as investing in the first years of the Pottstown Symphony as it had been newly constituted under William Lamb. Elsie Huff and Cory Schumacher were good friends and it was probably Elsie and her husband, Leonard, who, together with Bill Lamb, persuaded Cory Schumacher that this further development in Pottstown's musical history was worth her investment and financial support. At the very least the orchestra that existed during this phase of the history of the Pottstown Symphony was more a semi-professional and school related orchestra which served to provide opportunities for the best young players in the region. Thanks to the support of Cory Schumacher, this later development in its history was made possible. This can also be documented according to a 1953 report in the Pottstown Mercury of a birthday party held in Hershey, Pennsylvania for the then President Dwight Eisenhower that suggests the rivalry between the Pottstown Town Band under the direction of Mr. Lamb and the still young Pottstown Symphony. The Mercury reports: "William Lamb, Jr., director of the Pottstown band, meanwhile provided Pottstonians with [a] firsthand account of what went on inside the big tent, where some 8000 persons who paid $100 a-plate got a closer view of the Nation's top executive. A 25-foot high birthday cake was in the center ring of the tent.

---

[40] Information provided by Dr. William Nash in a telephone conversation with this author on 26 August 2012.

The Pottstown Band, which played from 4:30 to 7:30 p.m., was located in one of the two end rings. In the other ring was another string orchestra."[41]

With the body of evidence speaking for a much earlier founding of the Pottstown Symphony its origins in view of the later development of the ensemble following 1964 must not be forgotten here. The "idea" of the Pottstown Symphony seemed to remain in the consciousness of those few professional musicians living in the area. When it eventually folded and Mr. Morse was no longer controlling its fate, a chronology which this author believes to have come to pass sometime between 1955 and 1959, the memory of Pottstown's orchestra remained in the public memory. This can be seen even now, years after the death of the resurrected Pottstown Symphony, where, from time to time newspaper articles or letters or bloggers wish for the return of their orchestra but admit that it will never come back in its former glory. This "memory" must have burned especially bright in Mr. Lamb and the loss of interest in music caused by the lack of symphonic concerts in Pottstown must have weighed heavily on his financial and professional life. This, I believe, was the real reason for the resurrection of Mr. Morse's orchestra. However, it is evident that it is also the same ensemble, restored to life following a brief hibernation. In this sense, the symphony morphed from several organizations over many, many years. In any case, it cannot be denied that the musical life in Pottstown goes back considerably farther than 1964. Indeed, the primordial seeds of the Pottstown Symphony are to be found in the community long before the start of the Civil War.

At the time all this was occurring, Mr. Lamb had become the Music Supervisor for the Pottstown schools. He had already been director of the Pottstown Town Band and, after 1964, of the idea of the orchestra after Mr. Morse or his successor relinquished this role. However, no record has surfaced indicating who that successor, if any, may have been and at which point Morris relinquished his leadership of the ensemble. What is telling, however, is that Lamb continued Mr. Morse's practice and brought in students from Temple University's School of Music in Philadelphia and from the Curtis Institute to fill in the absent players and to strengthen the sections when it became necessary to do so. After all, despite the arguments of those on the symphony board that the Pottstown Symphony was traditionally a Pottstown-only orchestra, the ensemble's history tells an entirely different story. In fact, scholarship funding was made available to the most talented of these "foreign" students in exchange for their loyalty to

---

[41] "Ike's Gesture Impresses Area Resident". Pottstown Mercury from 14 October 1953.

the fledgling orchestra. Even at the highest levels within the body of orchestra musicians engaged to perform in Pottstown, one finds significant names associated with "foreign" orchestras. Most significant of these was the violinist and former concert master of the Philadelphia Orchestra, David Madison, who, according to the Philadelphia Daily News: "…also served as concertmaster for the Allentown Symphony, the Trenton Symphony and the Pottstown Symphony."[42]

This growing need to work with other, truly accomplished and professional musicians in the area was also served through the creation of the Pottstown Chamber Orchestra, an ensemble which existed between 1969 and 1971 and which engaged many of the string players from the Pottstown Symphony while hiring winds and brass as needed from both the Curtis Institute and from Temple University. The Pottstown Chamber Orchestra was an offshoot of the Pottstown Symphony in that it engaged some of the same musicians. This orchestra was under the direction of James Hoover who was also the music director of the then best choral group in the region, the Coventry Singers. What association, if any, the Pottstown Chamber Orchestra may have had with the Pottstown Symphony, aside from engaging its string players, is not known to this author.

At some point, Mr. Lamb's wife became involved with, first of all, the Pottsgrove school system and, later, with the Boyertown schools, both the Pottsgrove and Boyertown school systems being within a short drive of Pottstown. Especially Boyertown had already started to develop a significant string education program and Mrs. Lamb had been hired in Boyertown to teach elementary strings. She then moved from the Boyertown schools to a private school, The Wyndcroft School, also in Pottstown and continued her role as music teacher there, remaining in contact with string players she had taught and helping to guarantee their continued loyalty to the Pottstown Symphony within the framework of the orchestra's new-found tradition as a Pottstown-only ensemble. From that point forward, the Pottstown Symphony was internally an orchestra that fulfilled its need for personnel from some of the best musicians in the extended region but, outwardly, continued to be an ensemble only for locals.

It is interesting to remember, as a historical footnote, that during the time Mr. Morse was active as conductor of the Pottstown Symphony there had also existed a Little Orchestra Association in Pottstown whose Music Director was Raymond Elliott. Raymond Elliott has already been mentioned earlier as president of the 1st Federal Savings and Loan. This orchestra was

---

[42] Philadelphia Daily News. 27 July 1992. www.articles.philly.com/1992-07-27/news/26025460_1_violin-david-madison-philad…

created by Elliott in order to present concerts, from time to time, in the lobby of the bank but it was also known for its educational concerts which drew an audience of approximately 1500 children and for its repertoire, which included such potboilers as "Danse macabre", Johann Strauss waltzes and music by Handel. A recent conversation with Mr. Charles Clayton who had performed in the Little Orchestra Society and was also an employee of the bank at that time, confirms the interest the Pottstown public showed in live music performance during the 1950s and 1960s.[43] Also, in a notice in the Daily Pottstown Ledger dated February 04, 1909, there appears the following: "A new orchestra known as The Pottstown Orchestra, which will play higher grades of music with a full instrumentation, will be organized on Friday evening at the Y.M.C.A. The orchestra will not be connected with the Y.M.C.A., however. The orchestra will be under the direction of William H. Welser."[44] Following this announcement, the article mentions the names of 28 persons who had already committed to performing in this ensemble. From these early attempts to create an active orchestra culture in Pottstown and from the many supportive comments in the press regarding the Pottstown Town Band and other ensembles in the community, one wonders why Pottstown was never able to sustain a vital and creative cultural life. It must be remembered that this was an industrial town, populated by factory workers or blue-collar labor. At the end of World War II, Pottstown was home to major companies, among them Bethlehem Steel, Ellis Keystone Agricultural Works, the Pottstown Machine Company, Mayer Pollock, United States Axle, Spicer, Neapco Products, Doehler-Jarvis, Pottstown Plating, Pottstown Metal Products, Jacobs Aircraft Engine, Firestone Tire and Rubber, Pottstown Roller Mills, various dairies and firms producing agricultural products, Mrs. Smith's Pies and many more. The community was one of immigrants. "It is also important to remember that, up to about 1850, the Pottstown area was definitely bi-lingual, for German was as widely used as English. The old German Bibles and other publications of Christopher Sauer in Germantown still frequently turn up here today as evidence of their former use and currency. In the early days of Pottstown, the Borough, there were both English and German newspapers, although only one of the latter is now known."[45]

In "Living Places" an on-line biography and history of Pottstown, one finds the following interesting footnote: "By 1880, Pottstown had become Boom

---

[43] Telephone conversation between Mr. Charles Clayton of Pottstown and this author conducted on 03 October 2012.
[44] Daily Pottstown Ledger, February 04, 1909.
[45] Paul Chancellor, Marjorie Potts Wendell: *A History of Pottstown Pennsylvania* (Pottstown Historical Society. Pottstown, PA 1953), p. 129.

Town, U.S.A. The iron factories were attracting hundreds of workers from Philadelphia and beyond. John Ellis had built a factory to produce his Ellis Champion Grain Thresher, which was being shipped to practically every grain growing country in the world.

The <u>Montgomery Ledger</u>, Pottstown's home newspaper, reported that housing was in great demand. A real estate salesman reported that he could 'sell 25 houses in 24 hours if I had them to sell.' A builder who had just completed eight homes on North Hanover Street said he had 40 applications for them. The <u>Ledger</u> reported that on Saturdays, payday at the mills, crowds of men and boys gathered on the street corners and made it difficult for shoppers to pass. The paper editorialized that a police force was needed to deal with the problems of growth."[46]

At this point in its history, the community was a genuine melting-pot and the assimilation of its European heritage into the American mainstream would have also introduced a love of the arts and culture into the population were it not for other factors such as the Great Depression, xenophobic sentiments following the two world wars, the disappearance of most of the major companies from Pottstown in the 1960s and later as a consequence of the growing trend toward globalization of industry and of outsourcing. By 1999, when the symphony's first executive director was engaged, Pottstown was all but a ghost town. In 2008, when its second and final executive director left the scene, the town was a hotbed for crime, prostitution and poverty. At that stage in its decline, even the existence of the historically important Emmanuel Lutheran Church was endangered, its financial reserves depleted and its parishioners either dying off or having left the community in search of a better life. The local politicians seemed to take little heed of the impending tidal wave of insolvencies. It is probable that the externalization of the story that the Pottstown orchestra was a purely Pottstown product would also have had a decisive social benefit apart from its clearly commercial purpose. It would have provided the town with something of stature of which it could be proud. This pride, however, was never really echoed by those in Borough Hall and the miserably inadequate, commercial nature of Pottstown's pride, soon overtook any considerations of tourism or reconstruction.

Alone, however, the Pottstown Symphony's economically commercialized fantasy that required musicians to be recruited from those living within

---

[46] Living Places: Old Pottstown Historic District. Copyright 1997-2012. The Gombach Group.
http://www.livingplaces.com/PA/Montgomery_County/Pottstown_Borough/Old_Pottstown_Historic_District.html.

Pottstown would have hurt no one if it were not for the opinion the board of directors developed of itself as a "chosen people". This led to inaction, to a refusal to engage in the "demeaning" exercise of development campaigns and to an irresponsible denial of its continuing and never-ending stewardship obligations. Also the probable existence of rival or "parallel" organizations in the first years of the symphony's "official" existence seems to have made no impact on the official version of the Pottstown Symphony's history. Later, with the assumption of personnel obligations in the form of its first executive director whom the board dismissed for dubious reasons in 2002 or 2003 and to whom it had to pay significant damages to avoid a legal action by him, this tragedy became complete. It was this payment to the first executive director, coupled with the failure and unwillingness to fundraise, that contributed to depleting the orchestra's endowment from $250,000 to something amounting to about $40, all within six years. Subsequently, the very person who was entrusted with the management of this endowment fund in the latter years of its erosion, the wife of the headmaster of the Hill School in Pottstown and a member of its faculty serving in the office of the headmaster there, became president of the symphony board at the time the house of cards began to fall apart. I cannot with any authority, or in any sense of fairness towards her, report of any actions she had undertaken, neither prior to her appointment as president nor thereafter which were targeted to the reestablishment of the symphony's endowment. What makes this exceptionally tragic is her position of influence in the executive wing of one of the wealthiest and best endowed private boarding schools on the US east coast.

In the arts, this phenomenon is not so unusual and would have been easily remedied in Pottstown were it not also for the 20-year long perpetuation of this caste system through antiquated and self-serving governance policies. The then president of the board of directors who had a firm grasp on her position until the end of 2006, held fast to her post for these two decades and left behind, when she finally did depart under massive external pressure, a wake of debt, asocial behavior, board level incompetence and political quasi-incest.

However, the continuing history of the Pottstown Symphony required, in decades to come, a further subjective fine-tuning to keep the legend alive. After William Lamb's death, his successor, Porter Eidam, continued the tradition of hiring the best available musicians and music students from outside the region. Eidam was seeking to make a quality ensemble and to do so in a town the size of Pottstown with a then population of about 20,000 persons. In a community of this size it would have been impossible to otherwise maintain a symphony orchestra without the services of outside musicians. Sometime after Bill Lamb's death and after Eidam had assumed the reins of the orchestra, Porter Eidam created a working partnership with a Bill Schinstine who was first associated with the Pottstown schools and, later, owner of the S&S School of Music in Pottstown. Schinstine was a graduate of the Eastman School of Music and of the University of Pennsylvania and had performed with the Rochester Symphony, National Symphony, Pittsburgh Symphony and San Antonio Symphony orchestras. He had taught public school for 27 years in Pottstown before founding S&S Music and had worked with both Eidam and, earlier with Lamb and, himself a percussionist, brought strength to this section of the symphony. His partnership with Eidam later also provided Schinstine with extra income through lessons, sheet music, repairs and rental of rehearsal space although it is reported that an unhealthy and somewhat hostile rivalry existed between them which later resulted in Schinstine leaving the employ of the Pottstown schools. In 2002, following the death of Porter Eidam, who had repeatedly tried to reform this orchestra and its systems following the death of Mr. Lamb but who failed miserably thanks to the hardened political fronts and subjective historical infallibility against which he had to fight, a young woman assumed the role of music director there. She has been mentioned in the first chapter of this book as the first victim of the organization's melt-down. This new music director remained in her post until 2008 when she resigned with certain key members of the orchestra's board of directors and with others in a protest action which revealed the crumbling foundation on which the organization had stood all these years. For these six years, she worked diligently and creatively and built an orchestra in Pottstown that had become the envy of the entire region. Even the <u>Philadelphia Inquirer</u> had called the Pottstown Symphony the town's "note of distinction"[47] in 2007 in a lead article by the newspaper's music critic, David Patrick Stearns. Recording companies flocked to sign this orchestra to record deals and a major, international corporation took the ensemble under its wing as its "season sponsor" in the same year.

When this music director left, in 2008, the history of the orchestra changed yet again. Her name was removed from the narrative on the web site and from the official history of the Pottstown Symphony Orchestra and, in a grand gesture; the years between 2002 and 2008 were forgotten. As Pharaoh had condemned Moses, she was the prophet who was to be stricken from "every pillar and obelisk". It was as if her name was, never again, to be uttered.

---

[47] David Patrick Stearns: "Fully Professional – In Pottstown" The Philadelphia Inquirer. 01 November 2007.

Now, years later, having been forgotten in this context of history probably has had more positive than negative consequences for her. After she left, the orchestra's board furthered its deception by conducting what seemed from a distance to be nothing more than a sham music director recruitment campaign. My impression was that this was done to gain time for the board of directors and its leadership, to try and show the donors and the public that the board had everything under control. Eventually they did hire a music director, a young man from Philadelphia and conductor of a youth orchestra there who, as I learned, only was allowed to conduct one concert and whose planned, initial concert season was cancelled abruptly simply because the funds were not there to pay for it. However, the subjective redefinition of self, particularly for a publically-supported and tax-exempt organization as was the Pottstown Symphony, also destroys the ability of such an organization to evaluate and criticize itself and develop as an entity. This creation story may be a delightful fantasy. It comforts those closest to it and wards off threats or challenges coming from the outside world. However, it also denies that to survive and to grow as an artistic entity, these very challenges and their accompanying threats are what make such an organization resilient and flexible. The members of the board of directors of the Pottstown Symphony buried their collective heads in the sands of their own ignorance and, yes, of their own fears while, around them, the world was rapidly changing.

Think what you will of the need for persons or organizations to defend their own self-definitions. It remains the ability to redefine oneself that brings resilience to threats and teaches survival strategies. Organizations are also subject to Darwinian Theory. Organizations must also adjust and adapt to climate and to society. In its refusal to face the realities of its own development and of the development of the community and of the society in which it and its board of directors lived and worked, the Pottstown Symphony also proclaimed and sealed its own demise.

Whatever may follow in Pottstown in the years and decades to come, if, indeed, any artistic organization is foolhardy enough to attempt to establish itself there in Pottstown's climate of apathy, political corruption, criminality and poverty, its life-span will be, in part, determined by how it defines and copes with its own history. This is true anywhere, regardless of the social or economic climate or of political obligations in any corrupt or less corrupt society.

In its history, be it a history of almost 70 years (if we assume 1940 or 1948 as its creation date) or if we accept the given and biblical date of its creation as being 1964 (in the official version), this organization has blocked out segments of its past which could have cast a beacon into its future. The

Pottstown Symphony, in all probability, has no future any more. It has succeeded in its subjectivism at rationalizing itself into oblivion.

The questions surrounding the fate of Mr. Morse subsequent to the 1960's, until his death in 1983, seem all but lost to history. Also, no record has been found of any personnel lists belonging to the orchestra from this time, something that, most certainly, would have been circulated with any programs it would have performed in Pottstown and which the proud citizens of the town would have greatly enjoyed seeing and reading. There exist as well no concert programs or data of any kind prior to Mr. Lamb's first concert performed on 21 November 1964. That Mr. Lamb served as a player in Mr. Morse's orchestra can only be documented through oral accounts of his having done so. Chances are that, in a town the size of Pottstown, with its estimated 24 to 31 musicians, half of them being pop players or showing no interest in classical music, whatsoever, he not only played in the orchestra but, probably, also played a leadership role in it as owner of the most important music shop in the town. Curiously, the repertoire announced for that first concert of the Pottstown Orchestra under Mr. Lamb was a potpourri of classic hits which included Wagner, Dvorak, Gershwin, Richard Strauss and Emmanuel Chabrier. Building on the traditions laid down by Mr. Morse, Mr. Lamb was aiming high in selecting this repertoire. Such high aims require a historical foundation, something that could not have existed had the Pottstown Orchestra been started, from scratch, in 1964. It was Morse's building of this tradition and the training of players in the rigors of orchestra performance that made this community's dream a reality. The eradication of this rich tradition and the relegation of Mr. Morse to the dustbin of local history do not explain away the origins of what, over 30 years later, was to become a genuinely fine and respected orchestra.

It is my supposition that there may have been cartons of old Pottstown Symphony concert programs locked up in the basement or storage closet of Emmanuel Lutheran church or one of the other churches in the community but those which may have been stored at Emmanuel would have fallen victim to an unthinking housekeeping action in the church that forever destroyed access to any of this valuable historical data. It may also be that much of this same information is under lock and key in the home of Lamb's widow or of her daughter who once sat on the board of directors but we will never know. The symphony as it once was no longer exists as a tax entity. Its non-profit status was revoked by the United States Internal Revenue Service on 15 November of 2012[48]. As a professional organization hoping to enjoy the recognition of other, similar professional orchestras, it has no standing any longer. Its membership in the League of American Orchestras was terminated in September 2010 and its web site has been taken out of service and been up for sale and dormant for quite some time. Whether it will ever face reality and declare itself to be insolvent is a matter to be seen. As a vital cultural institution, however, it has ceased to function.

What cannot be explained, however, is the erasure of the years between 1940 and 1964 and, again, of the time from 2002 to 2008. This relegation of the uncomfortable side of its story to the waste basket of history is nothing less than an immoral distortion of that history and should be a warning to anyone who, in future, may wish to associate themselves with such an institution. Dictatorial and corrupt organizations and governments destroy evidence of their governance and of their history when allegations of possible criminality, in any form, be it malfeasance or misfeasance, are or could be imminent. They do so, as did the Stasi in the late 1980s in its frenetic action destroying 40 years of its documentation, to prevent knowledge of the unpleasant chapters stemming from their time in power from becoming known to others. Then there are others, the deniers of history, who, for example, excuse the Holocaust as mere fantasy. Such persons and institutions also rewrite their legends to retain the power structures they have built for themselves. The fall from power experienced by the board of directors of the Pottstown Symphony took over 20 years but it was a fall from power with, potentially, wide-ranging consequences not only for the orchestra and for its employees and musicians but for the community and the region as well.

What would have been the disgrace in acknowledging Kenneth Morse's contribution as presumed founder of this orchestra in 1940? The transformation of the ensemble from amateur to semi-professional to professional occurred over more than 50 years with the organization beginning to first take on its identity as a professional orchestra sometime after Porter Eidam took its helm. Under William Lamb, it initiated the structures which made Eidam's further development towards professionalism possible. Lamb continued the traditions established by Kenneth Morse and many of his practices but, shortly thereafter, with close ties to the Pottstown Schools. In 1971, the Pottstown Symphony was awarded its non-profit recognition from the United States Internal Revenue

---

[48] IRS Exempt Notice Select Check from 01 August 2013. The Pottstown Symphony Orchestra Association's 501(c)3 exemption was officially revoked on 15 November 2012 and posted to the web by the IRS on 11 March 2013.

Service with the granting of a 501(c)3 tax exemption. This latter development is Mr. Lamb's contribution. It would have honored his memory even more to have acknowledged him as the man who successfully risked these first steps to make a modern and professional ensemble out of a civic symphony and the acknowledgement of the Pottstown Symphony Orchestra's rich past would have brought recognition to the orchestra, the board and to the community. It represents a simply perverted sense of priorities that this historic wealth was seen in a negative context by this board. The truth in their past is something of which they could have been proud and which, as we will later examine, they could, much later, have also used to their and to the organization's advantage.

In future chapters we will discuss the singular elements that led to this fall from grace. We will also discuss the ramifications ideology had on the fate of the orchestra. In the case of the Pottstown Symphony, it was this power of ideologies over facts and the denial of the realities of the region and of the regional marketplace that helped to seal the fate of the symphony. The captains of this fate were the individual members of the board caught up in a destructively synergetic unity of purpose. In the following chapter, we will examine the board from a business, artistic and emotional perspective and attempt to exhume the long-buried prejudices, hatreds and emotional needs that led this board to act as irresponsibly as it did.

3. BANKERS, BROKERS, BRAGGARTS & BASTARDS

For anyone who has or who, someday, hopes to serve on a board of directors of a non-profit organization, the functions to be fulfilled through that participation and the obligations of each board member are variously defined depending upon which source you approach, the size of the organization and its financial stability or instability. Although most experts on board structure and governance acknowledge the social elements and camaraderie to be expected from such close associations, they also acknowledge the principle function of each board member to steward the organization and monitor the organization's fiscal health.

"In 1992, when the American Symphony Orchestra League (now League of American Orchestras) published a benchmark study of the financial condition of symphony orchestras, the prediction was that by the year 2000, the orchestra industry and individual orchestras would be in financial crisis if they did not significantly change the way they did business."[49] If it was even aware of the study at that time, the Pottstown Symphony Orchestra's board of directors seems not to have heeded that warning. At that time, with the orchestra surviving on a smaller budget, with a stable endowment and with little serious ambition to expand, it simply needed to examine its structures and its own self-governance, and to critically view how it managed itself and its methodology for and readiness to engage in fund-raising.

Instead, the opposite happened. I do not know what the scope of the ensemble's endowment fund may have been in the year 1992 but, by the year 2007, that fund had been reduced from $222,469 on 19 January 2000[50] to an approximate and pitiful $40 with no serious strategy having been created or implemented to refuel that fund.

In October 2005, the board of directors of the Pottstown Symphony consisted of 21 members plus a newly-hired executive director, a music director, an orchestra manager and a personnel contractor. The holders of these final four positions were regarded as associate directors and were without voting or other authority and served at the discretion of the larger, full board. There is nothing unusual in this structure except that the hostility that was beginning to form between this "staff" and the "board" with the board increasingly ignoring staff advice, and regularly using its monthly meetings as a vehicle to "verbally discipline" individual staff members,

---

[49] Dr. Thomas Wolf & Nancy Glaze: *And the Band Stopped Playing* (Cambridge, MA. Wolf, Keenes & Company 2005).
[50] Pottstown Symphony Orchestra Endowment Report of May 17, 2000.

mostly the music director and the executive director. This had built a wall of distrust between these groups. One cannot say that there was ever any significant misbehavior nor were there false decisions from the staff that would have given cause for disciplinary action. On the contrary, the disciplinary scolding was seen by individual board members as a way of keeping the staff under their collective thumbs. Especially the former president of the board, a woman who maintained a musical background but was actually superintendent of schools in a district not far from Pottstown, asserted her power over the organization by regularly disregarding the advice of the music director or executive director and by singling them out, from time to time, for a public whipping at board meetings.

The daughter of the presumed founder of the ensemble was also a board member at this time. Her professional role was as a music teacher in Pottsgrove, a school system just over the town line. As heir to the blood-line, she missed no opportunity to berate the executive director for what she deemed to be his inadequate fundraising activities although she had done little to fulfill her stewardship responsibilities.

Others on the Pottstown Symphony board were five teachers from various disciplines, an insurance company executive who also served as treasurer, various retirees, one politician, several musicians and one banker. This profile is relatively normal for such an organization with no objectives to grow or to assert itself on a larger stage.

The League of American Orchestras "Guide to Orchestral Governance"[51] delineates, however, several of the weak points in this composite and in the structure of the Pottstown Symphony board membership. On the average, 82% of the orchestra boards in the United States at that time limited the terms of the board members to three years while about 50% of the orchestras polled placed no limit on the number of consecutive terms a member may hold. This was the case in Pottstown with the board members playing musical chairs for years at a time. However, one has little difficulty here recognizing the board's inability to understand the association between artistic or institutional development and financial worth. Stories were told of individual board members having been appointed by the president simply because, one time, they had made a very modest donation to the organization. The rationale for such an appointment seems, from this perspective, to be the desire to create a body of hangers-on within the board, a set of dependencies which would guarantee to the then board president the votes she needed to continue her reign.

---

[51] American Symphony Orchestra League: Report: "A Guide to Orchestral Governance", New York 2005.

What substantiates this claim is an overview of the board makeup. On the average, orchestra board members are usually corporate CEOs or business owners who amount to, as a norm, about 21% of the board's composition. It makes sense for this weight to be on the side of money and influence since these men and women would also be in the best position to financially shore up an organization during difficult times as well as cultivate business associates who would become potential donors to the institution and, possibly, also future board members. They would also be expected to be critical in matters of business and of board leadership. In Pottstown, the category was filled by a mere 9% of the membership. On a national average, another 21% of those with seats on a symphony board consist of senior executives at corporations or banks. In Pottstown, this number was a little more than 13% which also included one local politician who, despite his claim of having influence in the community, proved to be completely ineffective in changing the town's attitude and in persuading the politicians to support the symphony. The most represented group on the board in Pottstown consisted of teachers who carried the weight of 32% of the membership. It is clear to see why. With the board president also belonging to this profession and with the desire to preserve the presumed educational value of the subjective retelling of its history, there would have been no better way to insure this continuity than to fill the board with those sympathetic to the teacher-led and classroom oriented directives of the organization's president. It is not surprising since the Pottstown Symphony had also fulfilled a serious educational role under William Lamb and since his daughter sat on the symphony's governing body. The addition of the remaining 26% of the board members, consisting of housewives, retirees, a musician in the orchestra, and a man whose professional life remained a mystery to everyone during his tenure, completes the picture of an organization that acted amateur and would have been better remaining so.

What changed all of this was the sudden realization that the Pottstown Symphony was getting into trouble and in sore need of a development person. Members of the board, probably the president and one or more of the other officers, engaged in conversations with the League of American Orchestras regarding this pending personnel decision and accepted what in retrospect was the flawed advice from the League that what they really needed was an executive director. Suddenly the idea of an executive director was seen by all as the magic bullet that would save the orchestra, ensuring the regular flow of funds from the countless foundations and grantors as well as private individuals who were just awaiting the opportunity to invest in Pottstown and its symphony.

An advertisement was released to the League's on-line web site with a salary of up to $75,000. The HR person who released this advert didn't think twice of the deception she had propagated in advertising a position for a salary the orchestra was not prepared to pay. The real salary was supposed to have been somewhere around $40,000 for which the new executive director was to fulfill all the usual obligations of that position plus be the sole fundraiser for the organization. It was clear that the board planned to sit back and wait for the dollars to rush in. The idea of stewardship was never addressed at this stage.

What complicated the relationship between the executive director, eventually engaged at a salary of $60,000 simply because he refused to come for less, was the fact that one of the board members, a school teacher, had been submitting grants applications from time to time and had been rewarded with a commission on the awards from each grant she successfully completed. I have heard a number of over $10,000 which she received for what I regard as an unethical compensation for a task that should have been part of her role as a board member. When the new executive director entered the field, she balked at communicating with him, seeing her golden goose threatened by this interloper who, after all, had only been hired to allow the board to sit back and continue to do almost nothing except meet and greet.

In January, 2006, the Pottstown Symphony reported working with an operating deficit of $33,759 based on a projected 2005/2006 operating budget of $431,594[52]. Already, the signs of a dangerous shortage of cash were evident. The orchestra had used its $20,000 line of credit with a local bank and taken out a loan for yet another $31,694 plus allowed itself to borrow $19,000 from the tenured orchestra manager. This produced a deficit picture of $70,694 in unsecured debt to be added to the previously announced $33,759 deficit. One can say with confidence that this debt was unsecured because the local bank had accepted the statement of the symphony board that the value of the orchestra's music library was far more than the amounts the bank was willing to lend. Whether this was fraud or a crass overstatement of the situation, the resale value of the symphony's music library could not have amounted to more than a few hundred dollars at that time. It was only years later that the bank was made aware of this situation but the horse had long left the barn and there was little one could have done at that late stage.

What was needed at the Pottstown Symphony was a strategy to win patrons and raise money and a board that cooperated with both initiatives. The ticket

---

[52] Pottstown Symphony Orchestra Association 2005-2006 Concert Season - Statement of Income and Expenses, June 2006.

sales were directed by a board member, a housewife and spouse of a retired pharmaceutical company employee. Later, he would also join the board and become its shortest-lived vice-president, trapped in a web of misrepresentation and intrigue directed against the music director. The methodology for these ticket sales was quite simple. The symphony had a telephone number which one would call and, with some luck, your ticket order would be taken by a living and breathing human being. Usually, however, you would be confronted by an answering machine that asked you to place your order and leave your credit card details and the tickets would be sent to you by regular mail. There was no patron directed organization of this effort and the presumption that one would reveal their sensitive credit card data to an anonymous answering machine was a state of affairs that was costing the symphony subscribers and public respect.

Shortly after he began his duties, the executive director's telephone began to ring in the office with calls from persons wanting to order tickets from him. He was not aware of this aspect of his position and the constant interruptions in the midst of grant writing, fundraising and season planning and issues with the musicians was a situation he couldn't allow himself to accept. In any case, there was never any decision made, neither from the board nor in consultation with the newly hired executive director that this job would also become part of his duties. I would insert here that this was a clear and initial sign that this board had little concept of both the functions and related responsibilities of an executive director. Additionally, nothing regarding such administrative chores was ever mentioned in his job description. He complained about this unannounced and disturbing attempt to shed the last shard of responsibility this board member had ever assumed and was met by a violent reprimand in the form of a public memo sent by the board president herself. Also, the executive director's success at securing a substantial grant from a major foundation with highly demanding criteria prompted him to remind the board of the increasing financial shortcomings and urge them to, simply, "…get their heads out of the sand." The urgency of the situation and his protests to the board that he had also received no information from and had no contact with the board member and teacher who had been writing grants on a commission basis met with a further reprimand from the then sitting board president. The board president wrote: "We are the ones paying both of your salaries (music director and executive director). We do not work for you…The money to pay for your salary has (sic) come through a dear friend of mine, who started this whole project to raise money for an executive director and to increase (the music director's) salary through a friendship with me. As president of this board, I would asked (sic) that you be respectful of all board members in your dealings at all times. You have had several short situations in the short time you have been here that you have offended many board members with your arrogant and abrupt directives...You were directed by (the HR board member), co-chairperson of the personnel committee to apologize to the appropriate people. To date you have not done so. This is just one example...Another very recent example was your snide comment to (the paid board member and former fund-raiser) at the last board meeting. She has been a dedicated member of the orchestra and board, and has raised a great deal of money for the PSO. You also owe her an apology...This orchestra has been in business for 42 years by the work and sweat of very dedicated people. Do not denigrate the work we have done over the years. It is ill-advised and extremely disrespectful."[53]

The thinly veiled message was simply that the new executive director was not wanted, that no professional advice or substantiated criticism, either from him or from the music director, would be tolerated or counted as being of any value and that the professional employees served at the whim of a board that knew little about running an arts institution and had no interest in learning.

One day later, on 02 March 2006, a second email was delivered by the husband of the woman who had so miserably mismanaged the ticket sales and had caused the symphony a loss of public support and public trust. He wrote: "Emails such as this may be your management style, bit I can assure you there are more acceptable ways to address this issue. To shotgun a punitive email to the entire board is counter-productive. There are some who don't get it, but then leadership has not made much of an effort to educate people on the transition of this organization from what it has been to what it is projected to become. To blanket a negative comment to the entire board will have an adverse impact on many who are actively trying to get this organization turned around. I personally take exception to your words and style, and hope you cool your arrogance just a little."[54] It is important to note that both the president and this board member were operating in the long standing Pottstown Symphony tradition of bullying the employees. It would have been quite enough, had there actually been an infraction of the rules, for the board president to have reprimanded the executive director but not in a public forum as had been her style for over a

---

[53] Internal Memo of 02 March 2006 from then sitting Board President to Executive Director with 20 persons on distribution.
[54] Board member Email sent to the Executive Director on 03 March 2006. This Board Member would later become the next Board Vice President and be dismissed or forced to resign due to unethical behavior with regard to personnel policies and the Music Director.

decade. The demeaning of an employee was paramount to her maintaining her superior role in the organization. It has also been reported to this author that this was the board president's style upon assuming the role of superintendent of schools and that many of her colleagues had lived and worked in fear of her wrath and of spontaneous dismissal at her hands. However, be that as it may, this second projectile fired from someone who had done nothing but contribute to the general malaise within the organization, was improper and singularly unprofessional. Both of these communications make obvious use of the single word, "arrogance". Arrogance in this circle was a metaphor for unwanted challenges or embarrassing questions. Later in this narrative, the word "governance" would become the operative synonym for board arrogance and oppressive behavior. At this stage in the devolution of the Pottstown Symphony, the introduction of foreign ideas or new concepts was, simply, unwanted and anyone who tried to break through the shell of the board's comfort zone was immediately branded as being "arrogant". At the risk of making too much of this point, this same gentleman board member, in this same email, promised to assist in future fundraising and contact the medical community in the region. He was also on the local hospital board. Nothing was ever done by him.

The issue here is that the need for dramatic action was being blocked by a board president who was alone interested in her social position and by a series of board members, all of them either fellow teachers or members of the church the board president attended, for whom the single priority was their presumed role and self-importance in the community. The fact that this organization had taken on employees and the responsibilities that go with so doing made no difference. This board operated under the misconception that people and employees could be thrown out of the organization on a whim. They had not learned the sad lesson from their experience with their first executive director, hired in 1999. A memo from him dated December 15, 1999 outlines an action plan which would place the assets of the symphony under a new corporate umbrella and in partnership with several other organizations in the region[55]. At that time, the plan would have helped to solidify the orchestra's financial future. However, it had one major flaw. The strategy in this action plan of December 15, 1999 failed to guarantee the already regal status of the board president and the matriarchy on the board. In my research, I have managed to locate records dating back to December 1998 which indicate that, even then, the orchestra, on a much

---

[55] Memo of 15 December 1999 from the Executive Director of the Pottstown Symphony Orchestra to the association's Strategic Planning Committee.

smaller scale, was living hand to mouth: "The treasurer presented and reviewed the current Dec. 16 report (bank bal. - $5,748.31), indicating that the balance will quickly be reduced by bills due shortly."[56]

Despite the presence on the board of a person who maintained she was a professional human resources manager, the Pottstown Symphony Orchestra Association's first executive director was dismissed sometime in 2002 for reasons which made no sense and, in the opinion of this author were invented to simply be rid of an unwanted individual. It is evident that the board and its officers had not considered the possibility of legal action initiated by the former employee. His threat to pursue just such an action resulted in the PSOA paying damages to avoid the probable lawsuit he had threatened. The music director of the organization, Porter Eidam, died in June, 2000. Thereafter, the first executive director had been dismissed and, following his threats to litigate, a payment had been made to him to avoid threatened action against the symphony. The endowment report of the Pottstown Symphony dated June 06, 2001 shows a systematic withdrawal of $60,000 from that account, initiated by the board in installments throughout the year 2000, beginning shortly after the symphony's first executive director was due to assume his role.[57] It may have been the case that this $60,000 withdrawal was used to pay the executive director's salary at the expense of any fundraising. The employment agreement with him called for "a minimum base salary of $43,000 per year, payable in equal monthly installments, with the first payment made on November 30, 1999."[58] It seems here that the board had decided to deplete its endowment funds to cover this personnel expense without any plan for fundraising or reinstatement of this amount having been discussed. In June 2001, the endowment fund had already been depleted at an alarming rate. Between December 31, 2000 and May 23, 2001, the value of this fund had lost almost $30,000. At that stage, without being certain of the exact date of the former executive director's dismissal and the sequence of events which led to this payment of damages, a sum, approximately equal to one year's salary for the then executive director must have been taken from the endowment to cover his claims and avoid a much more costly litigation. A restocking of this fund and acceptance of this experience as a learning process for the board would have gone a long way towards bringing this board into the world of professional music and of it accepting its role as stewards. It is important to again note that the board president in 1998 was the same board president who ruled the roost in 2006

---

[56] Minutes of the PSOA Board of Directors Meeting of Wednesday, December 16, 1998.
[57] Pottstown Symphony Orchestra Association Endowment Report of June 06, 2001.
[58] Executive Director Employment Agreement from October 28, 1999.

and her priorities were clearly nothing but the preservation of her status in the community. Whatever the symphony may have meant to her during her long tenure as president of the symphony board (1989 – 2006), it was not the first and primary reason why she held on to her board seat and this office for almost 20 years. As an aside, it is interesting to observe that the successful actions taken against the Pottstown Symphony Orchestra Association by its first executive director and as a result of his dismissal seem to have left a very bad taste in the mouths of long-tenured board members. As late as 2007 and 2008, he was still spoken about in highly derogatory tones within the confines of the symphony board. Certain individual board members who had worked with him correct the "official" opinion of this man as incompetent and lazy. From the perspective of this author, the Pottstown Symphony's first executive director seems to have been a highly accomplished, creative, dedicated and energetic employee. His misfortune was to land on the wrong side of the sitting board president and her circle coupled with the untimely death of Porter Eidam and the vacuum that ensued through Eidam's departure. The executive director quickly had to become a master of many tasks, some of which were not part of his mandate, in order to keep the symphony up and running. His absences from the office in his fulfillment of these vital assignments gave the board president the occasion to, unjustifiably, brand him as incompetent and effect the cancellation of his contract.

Following the death of Porter Eidam, the new music director took over the artistic direction of the orchestra in January 2002.[59]

In the memo of March 2006 to the second executive director, hired in 2005 after three years of amateur management in Pottstown and a further decline of the endowment fund and increasing debt, there is the following reference: "The money to pay for your salary has (sic) come through a dear friend of mine, who started this whole project to raise money for an executive director and to increase [the music director's] salary through a friendship with me."[60] This man was later referred to within symphony circles as "Mr. X". Mr. X was, in fact, a prominent attorney in the region who, for whatever reasons he may have had (and one of them could well have been his friendship with the sitting board president), organized a consortium of business persons for the purpose of engaging either a development director or, later as it proved to become, an executive director. This consortium was to provide for continuity within the orchestra in that it pledged to provide funds for the

---

[59] Evan Brandt: "Passing the Baton". Pottstown Mercury from January 06, 2002.
[60] Internal Memo of 02 March 2006 from then sitting Board President to Executive Director with 20 persons on distribution.

salaries of both the music director and the executive director for a period of several years. At this distance from the story, it is clear that the board president had never considered the ramifications of engaging professionals in arts management to manage the Pottstown Symphony. The advice from these professionals and the warnings of difficult times to come went unheeded by both the board and its officers. The single response from the board president and from much of the board itself was to attack those it had engaged to bring professionalism to the organization. It made little matter whether or not the advice from these persons, or from the personnel contractor or from other sources was good or pertinent to the problem. What mattered more than anything was the danger it presented to the board that it would lose control over the organization. With this board, the issue was always control. The absurdity of this need to retain control at any cost is demonstrated by the then board president's insistence that neither the executive director nor the music director nor, for that matter, the board itself was permitted to know the identity of "Mr. X". In this organization, neither the executive team nor the board, which carried the weight of liability for the organization, were given the information they needed to effectively and responsibly interface with the consortium head. It was not the advancement of the orchestra or the orchestra's relationship to its patrons and single ticket purchasers that was the issue in this episode with the, then sitting board members. It was an interloper threatening the structures which had provided immunity from criticism for a body of individuals who seem at this distance to have regarded their role as board members as nothing but a free-time activity.

However, there may have been other factors at work here that steered the clearly erratic and self-serving behavior of the then board president. It is fair to say that she saw herself as infallible in this role. It is this sense of infallibility and the gathering of slavish followers about her on the symphony board that created a climate where conflicting ideas had no place and persons with such ideas were unwanted. This was certainly the case with the first executive director who was clearly a thorn her side, as was also the case with other board members who, from time to time, posed a threat to her primacy. It is, nonetheless, quite likely that the behavior patterns she followed had much deeper, emotional roots. The German newspaper, Die Zeit, published a lengthy article on manipulative personalities in its issue of 14 August 2013. Citing the international financial crisis, the newspaper paraphrased an article appearing in the US magazine, Time, in which the CEO of Lehman Brothers, Richard Fuld, is considered to have been one of the top 25 individuals responsible for the devastating crisis which has set the world on its ear and cost countless lives from hunger, poverty and suicide.

Die Zeit cites Fuld from the Time article as "...a classic psychopath. Fuld, also known as "gorilla", threatened his critics in a company video that he would rip out their hearts and eat them alive."[61] This sort of behavior on the part of Richard Fuld prevented any criticism of his suicidal drive towards increasing corporate wealth at any cost from being stopped before it came to a catastrophic international collapse. With the Pottstown Symphony, the behavior of the board president was quite similar although much more refined. However, in the same article in Die Zeit the newspaper reports on a meta-analysis conducted by the US psychologist, Sara Konrath, consisting of more than 13,000 American college students. Shocking is that this study showed "...that the degree of empathy steadily declined in the years between 1979 and 2009 and fell most dramatically after 2000. The students showed an increasing inability to display sympathy for persons who do not seem to have the advantages that they enjoy or didn't seem to belong on the same rung of the social ladder. At the same time, asocial narcissism had increased during this period, especially in the previous 10 years."[62]

The consequences can be dramatic when those in authority refuse to accept normal and sensible control mechanisms. Aside from its fundraising responsibilities, a primary reason for having a board of directors is the availability of experts and, by their presence and through their interactions, the putting into place of a system of checks and balances that come from diverging opinions. When, however, there is draconian control over how one thinks and what one dares to express, these mechanisms cease to work and a climate of chaos is created in the image and likeness of one, highly narcissistic personality, who also carries the role of self-imposed primus in the organization. It is this narcissism, coupled with similar tendencies as reported upon by Sara Konrath in her study, which suffocated any efforts to change the diseased internal culture that had taken hold in the symphony and in its board. As the psychologist and expert on psychopathic behavior, Kevin Dutton, reported in his work, *The Wisdom of Psychopaths*, the psychopaths among us are not the bloodthirsty serial killers who mutilate women and eat children. These are the extreme representatives of this genre who, sooner or later, land in prison. "For Dutton these are the failures among the psychopathic population – the, by far, larger numbers walk about freely and are successful in their jobs since they command certain characteristics that they can well use in their careers. They regard themselves as grand and impressive, can be extremely charming and know neither scruples nor remorse nor fear. They do not shy from risk and know how to

---

[61] Die Zeit: „Wahnsinns-Typen". 14 August 2013, page 20.
[62] Ibid.

engage persons for their purposes. They are masters of manipulation."[63] In the case of the Pottstown Symphony, and for whatever reasons which this author fails to comprehend, the need for this board president to be the center of attention in all things did not compel her to also recognize the damage that would be done to her and to her reputation were the symphony to fail. It was a simple case of short-term self-adulation surmounting the need for long-term communal action.

Following the episode with the board member assigned to ticket sales, the second executive director went to work and created a system for on-line ticketing where the responsibility of the person assigned to tickets was simply to package them together and either mail them to the customer or have them held at the box office for collection on the evening of the concert. He presented this system to the board sometime in early 2006, several weeks following this memo from the board president and before the announcement of the new 2006-2007 season. The response from certain board members to this new idea was negative and hostile. The board member affected by this change, one who was doing this job in a less than satisfactory and decidedly unprofessional fashion, protested with the sentence: "…so what is left for me to do?" The executive director replied with a simple statement of fact, i.e., she could also get involved in fund raising. The idea that someone would call attention to the lethargy on this board and its responsibilities to and for the fiscal health of the organization at a time when the orchestra's debt was climbing and would soon be out of control, was a concept new to this board. Advice was never taken easily, especially from persons seen to be inferior such as employees, and the feelings of the board members were always more important than accountability and the responsibilities they carried through the acceptance and occupancy of a board seat.

The toleration of such behavior and the very existence of such questions posed by a person who, supposedly, served a leadership function on a symphony board of directors as well as in corporate America was highlighted in a radio broadcast entitled "Peter Day's World of Business" and moderated by Peter Day of the UK's BBC. This specific program, which this author first heard on October 19th 2013, was entitled "The World Turned Upside Down" and dealt, in part, with the glorification of autocratic behavior at the upper levels of management. Mr. Day remarks that "companies don't seem to care very much about the frustration they are

---

[63] Ibid.

causing."[64] To reinforce his premise, he also interviewed Marvin Bauer, thought by many to have been the inventor of the modern scheme of global management consultancy and partner in the McKinsey organization since 1933, as well as, in Los Angeles, Prof. Peter Drucker, an equally well respected authority on international business and management systems with over 60 years of international experience in this field. To the question as to whether business has changed very much, Mr. Drucker responded: "After almost 60 years of consulting, my basic emphasis that human beings are a resource and not a cost has had practically no impact in this country or in Europe. Everybody says people are our greatest asset then fires them…there is a glorification of the autocratic executive."[65]

However, this glorification of autocratic behavior coupled with psychopathic tendencies often to be found at the uppermost leadership level fails to explain why organizations such as the Pottstown Symphony board were often leaderless in themselves or were led in a fashion that led to the internal and external destruction of the organization and to the thorough demoralization of the employees. In an attempt to answer this question, Peter Day also interviewed the American cartoonist and journalist and creator of the comic strip, *Dilbert,* Scott Adams. Mr. Adams had been, himself, a captive of corporate America and this captivity and his perceptions of the hierarchical structures and leaderless systems that plague much of the business community (as well as the arts community in many cases) is at the core of the social commentary that comprises the *Dilbert* comics. Mr. Adams spoke of the obsoleteness of the famous "Peter Principal" and its further development into what he now calls the "Dilbert Principal". The core of this theory also touches the marrow of what was wrong in the Pottstown Symphony. In his interview with Peter Day on the BBC, Mr. Adams said: "…the most incompetent employees are singled out and promoted directly into management without their passing into that temporary "competent" stage and this actually makes sense in a perverse kind of way because, in the old days, the manager had to be the smartest one because the manager had to know how to be a manager plus understand all of the jobs of the people below him. But now, the smartest people have to be the people doing the work. You want the smartest person to be the computer programmer, the person doing the heart surgery, the person piloting the jet and you want your least intelligent person to be the person asking for status reports and doing team-building exercises and doing the hiring and firing…if you look at companies that have thrived, invariably they also have

---

[64] Peter Day: "The World Turned Upside Down" broadcast on the BBC, London, England, on 19 October 2013.
[65] Ibid.

the best product and, amazingly, many companies spend huge amounts of resources doing stuff that doesn't help the product directly like doing a team-work exercise to get together the finance group before the quality team pre-meeting. If you're doing that kind of thing, your company is doomed."[66]

As we delve further into this mismanagement structure that plagued the Pottstown Symphony we can ascertain that it was the *sine qua non* that motivated board actions and board decisions. The difficulty in such structures is to begin the shift in influence within the body of organization so that the source of any initiatives proposed for the good of the orchestra and for the organization would come from the bottom of the structural ladder and not be subject to the forlorn expectation that such decisions would be made and processes initiated by uninformed persons at board level, essentially also ignorant of the needs of an arts organization and, for many of whom, there had been no experience at any level in the corporate world.

The changes in this orchestra and in its management were an example of this shift and they proceeded more swiftly once the new ticketing system had been initiated but the front between the board and the employees grew to become a wall separating the interests of the board in maintaining its primacy from the hopes and wishes of the managers (music director and executive director) to make of the ensemble a successful regional orchestra. Earlier the board had approved a resolution where this orchestra was to strive for regional status.

In a draft of the Pottstown Symphony's Strategic Plan, dated May 04, 2008, the orchestra documents this as follows in its newly revised "Mission Statement": "The orchestra will provide and sustain a professional orchestra of the highest quality, and will actively promote the arts through music education, thereby enriching the quality of life throughout the greater Southeastern Pennsylvania region."[67] It is of interest here to note that the previous version of this statement, dated February 25, 2008, incorporated the phrase "in the Pottstown Tri-County region"[68] which was later replaced by "life throughout the greater Southeastern Pennsylvania region". Clearly this was a restatement of the board's wish to regionalize. The futile actions of this year in search of a new and regional name for the orchestra and its inability to change from its traditional adherence to Pottstown to a positioning within

---

[66] Ibid.
[67] Pottstown Symphony Orchestra, Planning Committee, Strategic Plan from May 04, 2008.
[68] Pottstown Symphony Orchestra, Planning Committee, Strategic Plan from February 25, 2008.

a regional context complete the picture of an organization that, clearly, was paralyzed by the fact that it saw no future for itself in this community.

The question remains as to how the board expected to realize any sort of transformation. With the accrued deficit having increased from approximately $70,000, including unsecured loans and lines of credit, to a projected shortfall of $178,000 in July of 2007 and with no fundraising of any consequence either planned or in the planning stage, there was simply no financial cushion to cover these costs. In an email to a board member regarding his position on the newly constituted executive committee and refuting his rightful assertion that, as chairman of the strategic planning committee he also was justified in participating in executive committee decisions, the new board president, elected in 2007, briefly addressed the ponderous debt the orchestra had already amassed. In this memo, dated July 13, 2007, she wrote: "Please keep your thoughts about this organization positive, it took a long time for the PSOA to get into the trouble it's in. It will take a long time to be where we all want to be, all of which will require a great deal of energy and patience from all of us."[69] At that late date, it seemed that the new board president and former head of the endowment committee had assumed the attitude of her predecessor. There was no genuine or ongoing fundraising being carried on and no obvious plans to initiate any actions in this area. One day later, the music director sent a comment to the executive director as follows: "I was utterly stupefied, horrified and made speechless by this statement. What does an emergency mean to this woman? $400K of debt...Is "patience going to pay your salary, mine and [the administrative assistant's]"[70] Months later, in a budget projection dated February 27, 2008, that deficit had increased again, this time to a projected $394,000.[71] Still there was no organized or effective fundraising. More will be detailed on this issue in a later chapter. It is mentioned here, however, since it seems to have been part of a strategy to re-"Pottstownize" the symphony and drive out, at very least, its executive director. In chapter four, the circumstances and consequences of this will be detailed as well as its history, a history which started in 2005 and came to an end in June, 2008 with the departure of the executive director and his return to Europe.

One thing is clear. By the time we reached January 2008, the board had deported itself on two fronts, the old guard with its allegiance to the previous president of 20 years and to her chosen successor versus an influential

---

[69] Internal Memo between Board President and Board Member dated July 13, 2007.
[70] Internal Memo from Music Director to Executive Director dated July 14, 2007.
[71] Pottstown Symphony Orchestra Budget Projections (July 2007 to June 2008), from February 27, 2008.

minority from that group who had begun to think differently about the organization and its responsibilities. The synergy that had developed between the music director and the executive director was a thorn in the side of many on the board. For many, a tug-of-war between executive director and music director would have been preferable and could have been used as a reason to fire the executive director. This didn't happen. Instead, there developed solidarity between both of them which infected many of those on the board who were seeking change. To this change of heart and the unanimity of purpose between executive director and music director, came several new board members coming from major banks, one from the music industry and one from an international medical systems conglomerate. One of these, the representative from the medical systems company which had also contributed a significant "season sponsorship" to the symphony, was also his company's director of internal audit. He was responsible for calling attention, in terms not to be misunderstood, to the perilous financial situation facing the Pottstown Symphony. The response of the board officers was to change the focus to governance and to try and rig decisions and policies to suit the will of the Pottstown crowd. One trick was to bypass the board as a whole and to try and give the decision-making role to the newly constituted governance committee. This committee quickly went to work impeaching one of the new bankers and "reforming" the governance of the symphony to where this committee, alone, dictated the course and future of the orchestra. What was so transparent in these governance rules was their unstated but well defined intention to create a climate of fear, where unswerving obedience to those few at the summit of the symphony's hierarchy was the only way to survive in the organization. What was going on here, within these governance structures, was a battle for that primacy at the cost of board unity and board-staff cooperation. A study prepared by the University of Alicante in Spain defines the proper purposes and direction that should be at the core of such governance reforms. In their article on business ethics they report: "...if managers want to perform corporate governance, not only do they have to know the problems related to staff expectations but they also must provide solutions to those problems, which in turn will progressively consolidate their managerial position...Another aspect to have in mind is that corporate governance is not a panacea for the resolution of group or individual problems within the firm. In this respect, no leadership style can solve alone all the situations in which a manager might find himself. Emphasis will have to be laid on one aspect or another depending on the specific department or individual concerned. An essential quality for those who have to develop this function lies in being able to diagnose the specific situation and knowing which of the possible ways or styles to deal with it is best and therefore should be chosen. In short, leadership by corporate governance goes beyond management, since it also includes the concepts of encouragement, help and service to others with the purpose of carrying out the organizational mission through ethically correct work."[72] These fundamental principles were never a factor in the Pottstown Symphony's governance structure and no attempt was created to establish an ethical workplace which would foster creativity and cooperation. At a time when the board also ignored its fundraising obligations, a factor which should have been the primary rationale behind any governance reforms, this development made the board as a group, de facto, a useless and superfluous organ.

In a memo of January 01, 2008, a board member who had, long ago, begun to realize the consequences of the direction the orchestra had now taken and the dangers to the ensemble and to its future that were coming from this adherence to the past and past policies and to presumed self-importance, initiated an action, together with an attorney and several other board members, to unseat the president and vice-president and to try and steer this organization from the rocks of its own self-destruction. The initiative failed due to the cowardice of one board member, a banker whose employer held much of the PSOA's debt and to intrigue and impeachment and stonewalling and a strategy that was far from aggressive enough to impact on the then leadership.

The board recruitment strategies initiated since late 2006 also served to do little more than perpetuate the ancient tradition of self-importance and power. Yes, the strategic planning committee did create a system that would result in the abdication of the former president of 20 years but this milquetoast document refused to acknowledge her accountability for the increasing debt, the inactivity of the board, the questionable personnel policies she had initiated and the dangerous degree of internal stagnation that had befallen the ensemble. Instead, this person was declared an honorary board member and the new statutes were so written that, within the short span of several years, she could return to the symphony board a second time and potentially resume the role of president. Her successor, a woman mentioned here as spouse of the headmaster of the Hill School in Pottstown and member of the faculty there, was woefully incompetent. She motivated neither the symphony's staff, nor the symphony board and she categorically refused to use any of her contacts within the Hill School to leverage in the interests of the symphony and its finances. In 2007, several

---

[72] Juan Llopis, M. Reyes Gonzalez & José L. Gasco: *Corporate Governance and Organizational Culture. The Role of Ethics Officers.* Department of Business Organization, University of Alicante, Spain.

wide-ranging fundraising strategies and motivational plans were developed by the executive director and, in special meetings, presented to the board. At first, the new president refused the executive director the right to even make those presentations. She was more impacted by the importance of the chain-of-command than by the necessity for action at a time when the tragedy could have been avoided. In summer of 2007, that meeting finally did take place but the board failed to react. Even the new vice president, a drama teacher in the region with the interesting license plate designation, "Drama Queen", gave nothing but lip-service to the plans presented by the executive director. Nothing happened at all. The election of a graduate of the Arts and Business Council of Philadelphia's "Business on Board" program to the board in summer 2007 seems from this distance to have been more of a strategic stroke against any reform that would be of any genuine or lasting benefit to the orchestra. The man proved to be a despot, a bully and carried on in the ignoble tradition of the previous and short-lived male vice-president who suddenly left the board after December 2006 after having misrepresented himself in a personnel action and orchestra musicians' survey designed to find a reason to dismiss or discipline the music director. Many also shared the opinion that this new appointee displayed dangerously aggressive tendencies. He seemed to enjoy his occasional and rabid attacks on the music director, a petite woman, but shied away from any direct attacks on the executive director who, clearly, could fend for himself. The behavior of the sitting board president and of her vice president during these attacks was exactly that of the former president. She passively sat back and offered no protection to an employee who was clearly being abused. It was clear that these attacks had been planned and that she, as were her predecessor and the others of her board officers, was in full agreement with this degradation of either the music director or, in one other case, of an elderly and active board member who simply disagreed with their proposals and policies. In short, the board president no longer acted in the interests of the employees and she refused to recognize her role as their supervisor but also as their protector. A jungle atmosphere had taken over the board of directors.

The political landscape in Pottstown's orchestra was now working against the orchestra itself. Members of the board, including several proudly and openly asserting their role as "conservative thinkers" buried themselves in their stoic interpretation of conservative notions of right and wrong and "pushed-back", in their own words, against any progressive trends that may have brought help to the organization. The chronically bullying member of the board teamed up with the most innocuous of these, an investment advisor who took offense at anything and anyone who disagreed with him and, together, they created a fortress mentality against new ideas and general change, a parallel to which can be seen today in the ideological war being waged among factions in the United States Congress. The Pottstown Symphony had become an institution incapable of movement of any kind, internally or externally. The name change project had been stopped by the summer of 2008 and the orchestra started branding itself in 2009 and 2010 as "positively Pottstown". The historical circle had been completed and, as stated in chapter two of this book, the subjectivism of its history had sealed its fate.

Had one member more of this orchestra board stood up and been willing to recognize the fatality of the fundamentally bad decisions that had been made, internally, within the clan of this newly devised governance dictatorship led by the bullying "Business on Board" graduate and self-appointed "king" of the symphony, this orchestra may have had a chance at survival. At the very end, the banker and creditor who had supported the forced abdication of the board and who had the most to lose were the symphony to declare itself insolvent and who had promised his wife, then dying of cancer, that he would rescue the symphony, became its biggest betrayer. He betrayed himself, his community and his responsibility to the employees, to his employer and to the musicians themselves. The other banker had, long ago, lost his nerves and buried himself in his personalized uncertainties. Others, among them the creative director for an advertising firm in the region, the retired logistics manager from a pharmaceutical firm, the music director, the executive director, an important musician in the area with copious funding contacts, the head of an audio company in Philadelphia with contacts to that scene, a former vice-president of an important bank in the region and the senior auditor of a major medical products company, all resigned or, in one case, had been impeached. They had been outnumbered by this one change of heart, by this slavish and senseless adherence to a long failed tradition.

The behind-the-scenes role of the former board president in this drama is not to be doubted as is the probable supporting role fulfilled by the infamous Mr. X, detailed here earlier as the presumed donor who would use his contacts and his consortium to bring the Pottstown Symphony into the new millennium. When, in late 2006, the executive director and music director learned that the promised fund to insure their positions had, suddenly, dried up, the reasons for this were clear. Failing all other methods, the former president of the board would go out with a bang and take both the music director and executive director with her. The employees would become the scapegoats and the deposed board president seen as the long-suffering victim of employee disloyalty and unprofessionalism. Legally, the employees would have to accept their terminations, having been fired for lack of financial support. The disappearance of that support would be cleverly traced back to the employees themselves. They had cost the symphony the support of the donors with their intrigue and their long tolerated, arrogant behavior. From this perspective, this lack of funds was clearly a strategic stroke to rid this orchestra of unwanted and unloved persons. The stroke failed when, discovering the impending blow to their positions, a discovery which, incidentally, was accidentally made by the music director and had not been communicated to either employee by any member or officer of the board, the executive director resigned and assumed a new position in Europe.

The title of this chapter, "Bankers, Brokers, Braggarts and Bastards", sadly details the makeup of this symphony board from the late 1990's to the end of its existence in 2010 or 2011. There were, however, others on the board who do not fit this designation and who were motivated and risked much to try and save the institution. This book is dedicated to one of them. What none of the reformers in this organization had realized at the time was the incredible power and influence of those promoting the existing inertia. The political winds were against any reform. The influence of the former board president went so far as to openly blame the music director and executive director for being at the root of the problems in the symphony. Meanwhile, no fundraising was conducted, the personnel policies were flawed, the board devoted countless and unending meetings, often lasting three or four hours or longer, to topics that should have been dismissed out of hand and the inertia continued. Comments made about respect to be shown to the board were senseless evasion. The attendance at board meetings, mandated for both the executive director and music director, proved to be tests of self-control. They were often attacked, rabidly, by isolated board members, often without reason. There was no respect shown to the staff at all. The assistant treasurer, a board officer, at one point, commented to the executive director that, and I paraphrase here: we are the board and we can do no wrong. You have only to do what you're told! It was in that climate that the Pottstown Symphony operated.

Also present on this board was the troubling xenophobic positioning of many of the board members, especially of the former president and her clique. The second executive director was a dual-national and his partner a German citizen in the USA on a Green Card. At home and, as well, also in public, their language mix varied between English and German, both of which they spoke fluently, and he often used his language skills in the office when dealing with potential European clients. In several cases, the symphony benefitted from this mini-internationalism but much of the board viewed these abilities with suspicion. In a region where, not a century before, the population was bi-lingual and in a town which always prided itself on being a mini melting pot, the hatred of anything foreign was a disgrace to the town's history. However, to be fair, this hatred or distrust was also applied to those who might have come from Philadelphia or from New Jersey or, heaven forbid, from far-away New York City. The members of the board of the Pottstown Symphony simply didn't travel and, when they did, it was either within familiar territory or on escorted cruises where they were protected among other Americans or friends who travelled with them. This was a group of people with little curiosity and no ideas. To them, anything new was immediately suspect and anything suspect was discarded out of hand. In this climate, anyone from the outside had no chance. Such a person, coming with new ideas, was and would always be "arrogant". The arrogance, however, lay in the eyes, the mind and the prejudices of the beholder.

However, perhaps most telling of all is an instance which took place in the waning days of the executive director's and music director's employment by symphony. Hearing from the music director that she was about to resign if there was not an immediate improvement in the situation and steps taken to stop the abuse of employees, the then president of the board went to the executive director and asked him if there was any substance to this threat made by the music director and what his plans would be if the music director should quit. The discussion gravitated to the complaints that all the employees had expressed, that their security and their livelihoods were threatened by the present fiscal irresponsibility. The executive director, whose partner suffers from an advanced stage of a serious eye disease and who, without proper and regular treatment, would quickly go blind, brought this unending financial insecurity up to the president as an intolerable emotional burden. He complained that his partner needed this certainty of knowing that he could cover her medical costs, including those involved with the treatment of her eye disease, and that the stability of his employer was key to this security. Without hesitation, the response of the board president personified the very asocial attitudes that had made this board so ineffective. She coldly said to him: "well, she's going blind anyway". With that single sentence, one can summarize the decadence that was at work among the members of this board. However, there is yet another story which further confirms this unwillingness to accept the board's responsibility for its decisions and actions. In the employment contracts with the Pottstown Symphony there was a commitment made by the board to provide to both the music director and to the executive director medical insurance which would also include coverage for dental treatment. During his initial term with the symphony, the executive director had been in possession of a dental insurance card which he surrendered back to the organization upon leaving its employ in December 2006. When he returned, in July 2007, he inquired after several months about his new card. At that point, he was in need of dental treatment and this insurance was guaranteed to him in his employment contract, signed earlier that same year. The response of the then assistant treasurer, an executive and partner with a local insurance brokerage company, was to dismiss this breach of contract with the phrase: "we haven't paid the bill for years".

In the following chapter, we will discuss the problems with the staff and its unwillingness, at first, to genuinely see the dangers to which it was exposed. We will examine the trusting attitude of many of them and the eventual division among the staff into adherents of reform and hangers-on to the old traditions. Later, we will look at the interplay of the musicians and the staff and the intrigues carried on between certain board members, the orchestra musicians and the American Federation of Musicians over the desired dismissal or degradation of the music director.

With this profile, nothing could have saved the Pottstown Symphony except the realization that its board structure, its immovability and its slavish adherence to useless traditions and the aloofness to be found among certain of the members of its board, had kept it from growing and maturing. The use of the school systems in the region or of a church congregation as a recruitment center for new board members or the granting of a seat to someone who, one time, donated $1,000 to your cause and did nothing thereafter for it, was failed logic carried to absurdity. The need to recruit from "their own kind" condemned them to incestuous dependencies. The child they produced, the symphony, was physically, morally and emotionally handicapped. The role of the board, its failure to be self-critical, to act as a business should and must act and to cast aside its petty prejudices in the interests of the ensemble finally lowered the axe onto the neck of the orchestra. It was simply suicide. The correct response to the question asked by the board member who lost her prized and self-important role as ticket guru in 2006 and the recognition of the meaning of that response by all may have gone a long way towards saving this orchestra. That answer was, simply the old and repeatedly proven adage that should control governance and stewardship among non-profit boards: "give, get or get off".

4. INTERPERSONAL RELATIONSHIPS

The Board's Attitude towards the Staff and towards itself

Maria Antoinette, the Queen of France prior to and during much of the French Revolution, is reputed to have replied to protests against hunger within the country's population with the immortal phrase, "let them eat cake". History also tells us that it was this phrase and the depersonalization of the French citizenry that led to both the revolution and contributed to its impact on public sentiment, to her falling victim to the guillotine. As with many such societies where the burden on the population or, in this case, on the employees of the Pottstown Symphony, increased steadily not for reasons of organizational development but in order to preserve the two-class system, the discontent of that same population or group of employees in its impatience at the status quo eventually reaches a critical mass. In politics, this critical mass can result in a regime change, a revolution or simply the election of the opposition political party.

In the case of the Pottstown Symphony the irregularity of its hiring practices, the infrequency of its hiring at all and the slender nature of its available staffing delayed any sort of organized rebellion from within the ranks. In 2008, the Nonprofit Finance Fund would also cite this problem as a deficiency and causal aspect of the Pottstown Symphony Orchestra's problems.[73] Also, the idea that for decades the board did everything and had traditionally done everything needed to administratively, but not financially sustain the orchestra and that no task from the sale of tickets through the mailing of season announcements and subscription renewal information or any other chore was beyond the scope of the "volunteer" board, contributed to the uncertainty accompanying any new hire.

The first of the recognized music directors, William Lamb, although de facto a "hired" employee was also the much touted founder of the Pottstown Symphony. His role as an employee was overshadowed by the dubious myth of him as creator of the orchestra and as the one who brought classical music to Pottstown. Mr. Lamb's successor, Porter Eidam, had a different role. Yes, he was recognized by the board as the carrier of the torch which had been passed to him by Mr. Lamb but he also arrived on the scene at a time when the influences and persons pushing for matriarchal control of the organization had begun to take a stranglehold on the orchestra.

In 1991, the composition of the board of directors showed a balance of male and female members, 10 of these being women and seven being men. By the

---

[73] Nonprofit Finance Fund report from March 2008.

time the organization collapsed in the year 2010, this balance had been retained but the size of the board had been reduced to a mere eight persons, less than half of what it had been only nine years before. Time and again, qualified persons from the region had refused the offer of a seat on this organization's board. The smallness of this board, the constitution of which should have led to speedier and more flexible decision making, resulted instead in chronic stagnation. The third president in this succession, the drama teacher and a former vice-president spoken of in a previous chapter, liaised with the bullying board member also spoken of earlier who, by this time, had become the board's vice-president. Together with the new treasurer, a member of the "conservative" group which had established itself in the organization, they carried the weight of decision and authority. The organization had lost all contacts to the music business and to any semblance of professional guidance. It had become a purely amateur organization purporting to be a professional one but without the solidity, commitment to solidarity and the experience or contact to experienced advisors outside of the region it would have needed to succeed.

As early as the tenure of Porter Eidam, this trend was beginning to bear fruit in the Pottstown Symphony. Mr. Eidam delivered a report to the board of directors on 19 November 1997 in which he rebutted the personal and professional attacks on him which had been delivered at a previous board meeting for cost overruns following a Broadway Pops concert. He devoted five pages to a minutely detailed narration of the circumstances behind these extra costs. Nowhere did he transfer the burden of blame to another except, in his conclusions, to highlight a philosophy and course of action at the board level that would later lead to litigation against the board.

In his "Final Statement" Mr. Eidam writes: "…Some of the override was my responsibility and mine alone. Most, however, was not. For example, I had no control over the cost of music, except to eliminate pieces. (But then…whose solo do I eliminate, and what does that do to program continuity?) Each of the elements fell into place not all at once, but by "dribs and drabs" so as not to seem so significant. By the time realization set in, it was too late to do anything. While several people were aware of the "goings-on", until the October Board meeting, no one questioned anything. The vehemence demonstrated toward me at that meeting came as a complete surprise! I do wish that someone would have shared the concern so I could have prepared a formal report prior and thus not have been subjected to a "blind-sided" attack. This report could have been much more succinct and perhaps the two-hour "feeding frenzy" in which I was the main entrée could have been avoided."[74]

In 1997, the same board president, the previously mentioned former superintendent of schools, was well into her tenure with the Pottstown Symphony. This was her style and became the style of personnel management that the board had adopted and which it would aggressively pursue until the organization was forced to close its doors. You will notice a conciliatory tone in Mr. Eidam's report. He must have been accustomed to such broadsides from this board. In this organization, such frontal and surprise attacks on the staff had become the usual way of managing personnel issues. The employees, from the time of this barrage in 1997 until the resignations of the music director and executive director and, indeed, beyond until the year 2010, were repeatedly held hostage to their fear of such massed attacks on their person and their professionalism.

However, this policy, if one may call it so, was not only restricted to the dealings between the board and its employees. As the strategy of frontal attack became established, these attacks were increasingly used against fellow and unpopular board members. In 2007, a self-appointed impeachment committee consisting of members of the governance committee unilaterally carried on an impeachment action against one of the leading board members, a banker and probably the most active fund raiser in the organization aside from the executive director and the music director. The circumstances behind this were, if anything, childish and showed the sensitivity of this board to any criticism from inside or from outside its ranks. A memo had been circulated among the accused board member, the music director and the executive director in which the board member, showing his frustration at the lack of fundraising, leadership and vision (all points which reflected a realistic view of the existing situation) expressively vented his discontent. For reasons which are difficult to understand at this distance, this memo acquired one or more additional names on its distribution and, therefore, became known to others on the board. It would have been the simple and adult thing to do had the board or the members of it to whom this memo referred simply swallowed their anger or, perhaps, spoken to this board member directly. In all likelihood, he would have apologized and everyone else involved in the incident, a genuine tempest in a teapot, would also have apologized and it could have resulted in a better understanding within the organization. However, that was not the way in the

---

[74] Porter Eidam: Report to the Board of Directors of the Pottstown Symphony Orchestra Association from the Music Director dated Wednesday, November 19, 1997.

Pottstown Symphony. Without the knowledge or the approving votes of the full board of directors (only the board president, the treasurer and assistant treasurer, the "Business on Board" member, the executive director and music director and, for some reason, the art director, were on copy) and without any form of disciplinary process having been voted upon or established within the organization, neither with respect to board members nor to the staff, this self-appointed impeachment committee sent the following memo to the "offending" board member: "You are hereby notified by the executive committee of the Pottstown Symphony Orchestra Association that a grievance, seeking your impeachment as a director, is filed against you for harmful and offensive behavior toward other board members, showing a malevolent attitude that is considered injurious to the morale and mission of the Association. And, that you did violate certain board-staff lines of authority and communication by directly discussing with, or making it known, to certain staff members your malevolent attitudes and derogatory and offensive opinions. By these actions, you have breached the board-staff integrity and your opinions and actions, both written and verbal, harmfully undermine the work that this board has undertaken to satisfy the mission of the association…Action taken by the board in any impeachment proceeding shall be conclusive and final…You are hereby notified that you are suspended from board meetings, committee meetings, vote (sic) participation, and any business (financial, or otherwise) pertaining to the Pottstown Symphony Orchestra Association, pending final outcome of this action."[75]

Without reference to any knowledge the full board should have had of such an impending action, the board president, wife of the headmaster of the exclusive boarding school in Pottstown, had simply taken it upon herself to demand that this "offending" board member resign his seat. This was done, presumably in a telephone conversation, on 26 September 2007. In fact, the executive committee of which this board president was also a member, had given itself this authority without full board approval in an attachment to the minutes of the 19 September 2007 board meeting. This "attachment" outlined the impeachment procedure and was dated one day prior to this telephone conversation with the "offending" board member. This document contained, among others, the following clauses: "Any Member may be suspended from the Board/office by majority consensus of the EC (executive committee), pending further action" and "complaints or a formal written grievance, accompanied by all available supporting facts and evidence

---

[75] Impeachment Defense Response to Filed Grievance. Memo of the Vice-President of the PSOA from 28 September 2007.

against a Member, must be presented to the Executive Committee (EC) through the President, or their designee, and endorsed by five (5) Directors in good standing."[76] Especially regarding point one above, it is doubtful that, in open discussion, the executive committee would have found "five directors in good standing", all who would have agreed to such an action. This leads to the conclusion that this initiative, announced only one day before the demand was made upon this board member that he resign, that this was nothing more than the planned dismissal of an individual using the methodology of a kangaroo court. As preamble to the previous cited memo sent on 28 September, the following rationale was used to justify what was nothing but a rogue action by a minority which had assumed a self-appointed authority to regulate the opinions and freedoms of its fellow board members: "Because of the embarrassing and serious nature of the information that came to the executive committee's attention through the issuance of the grievance against you, the opportunity to resign respectfully was given and, in so doing, not have this information made public. On Wednesday, September 26, 2007, you refused to accept this alternative [of] the president of the Pottstown Symphony Orchestra Association."[77]

Where was the rationale here? What was this thinly veiled threat to make this action a public one and with what authority did this group presume itself empowered to take such an action in the first instance? Despite what one may or may not have said about the style and language this board member may have used, the fact remains that there was not and had never been any procedure for the dismissal or impeachment of a board member, that the topic of this impeachment, or of any impeachment at any time, had never been debated at the full-board level and that the response of this committee was nothing more than an attempt to rid themselves of someone they didn't want to have in their ranks. He was unpopular because he was critical and he was active and he brought to the organization a financial wisdom and creativity foreign to this board. It also remains to be said that this supposedly offensive email which had purportedly violated "board-staff" lines of authority had not been sent to the administrative assistant, to a secretary or to a non-decision maker in the organization. Instead, and resulting from the synergetic development which was beginning to emerge between certain portions of the board and the executive staff, this email had been among this board member, the executive director and the music director, each of whom held a seat on the board and each of whom regularly attended board and committee meetings as a non-voting member. Nothing

---

[76] Pottstown Symphony Orchestra Association Procedure for Impeachment dated 25 September 2007.
[77] Ibid.

in this memo was a secret to anyone in this circle. Instead, what the committee displayed by this unilateral action targeted at dismissing one of its own was a serious and unhealthy degree of narcissism. This self-idolatry at the board level and, particularly, among the members of the executive committee who initiated this impeachment procedure, showed a dangerous belief on the part of those initiating the action that they were infallible in matters of policy. In short, they took it upon themselves to pronounce a verdict *ex cathedra* with the failed presumption that the entire board would accept this verdict and without question. Slowly, this committee and these few members were approaching a state of being that could be described as "ordained". In crossing this threshold this board had entered dangerous territory and it had ceased any longer to bear the right of calling itself a democratic institution. De facto, it had started a process towards violation of its own statutes and dismissal of the reason for its existence.

More important, however, is the fact that the attorney for the Pottstown Symphony Orchestra Association did nothing to stop this witch hunt. He was copied on this announced impeachment action and one would be relatively safe in suggesting that he was probably also consulted on it although there is no evidence to show this directly. However, as the legal counsel for this organization, it would have been his duty to have informed this committee that it was treading a dangerous path. This he did not do or, if he did, there is no record of any such counsel and no objections were raised at subsequent board meetings where protests against this impeachment without full-board approval and without an impeachment or disciplinary structure in place, were vocally expressed. In other matters, there have also been instances of questionable ethics which this attorney has upheld. Especially in the realm of fundraising and donations and in the assignment and distribution of restricted funds, his sense of right and wrong, ethical and unethical behavior seemed to be operating on a low flame. However, this is a topic for a later chapter in this book.

The accused board member, in a memo to the entire board and to the staff, resigned on October 1, 2007 but that was not to be the end of the story. It was this instance and the usurpation of power by a minority, a "rogue board" as it may be called, that set in motion a rebellion that would lead to the dissolution of the organization.

At the next board meeting, a long-tenured board member and one of those most offended by this action, distributed an article to the entire board which had been taken from the on-line site, Board & Administrator, in which was reported the actions of a rogue board chairperson. This long-standing and now-protesting Pottstown Symphony Orchestra Association board member was the first to recognize the rogue action of the minority. He was the first to signal the alarm and to warn of a takeover action and of the drive to turn this marginally democratic board structure into an organization led by a few despots. Here is a brief excerpt from this article which he gave to each and every one present on that Wednesday evening and it reveals a situation that was beginning to develop within the Pottstown Symphony. "I have a rogue board chairperson on my hands, and he's intent on taking complete control of the organization...Without my knowledge, the board chair recently hired an assistant administrator for the organization, He then hired an attorney, who will report to him directly. The chair's intent is that the attorney will consult directly with the board chair, at the exclusion of the full board and myself (sic)."[78]

This is what had begun to happen in Pottstown. The abusive board member who had come from the "Business on Board" program had worked himself into a position of authority and was acting in a unilateral fashion, exerting untoward and destructive influence on the already weak and indecisive board president and on the vice-president.

As reported earlier, the executive director had been recruited in 2005 thanks to a consortium of business people led by the head of the law firm that employed the Pottstown Symphony's attorney. It has also been reported that motivated by the changes the executive director had made in the organization, changes which led to increased audience numbers and better marketing and public outreach, the donations to the consortium that was supposed to pay his salary and benefits package for a period of several years had suddenly stopped. This fund had all but vanished and he and the music director were facing a sudden dismissal or, better said, the music director was facing her position being reduced to a part-time status without benefits and the executive director's fate would have been certain and immediate termination. He had no choice but to leave and under circumstances that would not damage his life, career and family.

The departure of the executive director in December 2006 left a vacuum in the organization and there were certain, highly influential board members, who were quite glad to reconsider rehiring him when it became known that his position in Europe was also in danger. He had taken a job in Vienna without looking closely enough at the seriousness of the organization and had discovered, too late, the nefarious and deceptive nature of the organization's leadership and its almost total lack of available operating capital. He resigned the position in Austria after three months and let it be known in Pottstown that, although he had other offers, he would consider returning. The logic was not to climb from the frying-pan back into the fire

---

[78] *Board & Administrator*, Jeff Stratton, editor. Vol. 20, No. 11, from July 2004.

but that the developments within the board had introduced powerful elements of professionalism coming from the music business and finance sectors and had introduced critical and professionally experienced voices to the operations of the board. The deciding factor that certain of the more critical board members with significant business backgrounds were also beginning to see the dry rot in their organization, brought hope, confirmed to him by the music director, that the Pottstown Symphony could finally take advantage of a modern and flexible management style.

However, as before, there was the problem of how to pay the returning executive director's salary. This time around, however, there was no consortium to pledge to cover this cost and, as usual, the board engaged in no significant fundraising to meet the expense it was about to assume in bringing him back. He had agreed to return at the same salary and benefits package level and with an initial contract term of four years. There was no endowment to shore up these costs and the symphony was already approaching a projected level of liability amounting to $140,000 at the end of 2007.[79]

Simply and practically stated, the responsible solution to this dilemma would have been to either operate without the return of the executive director or, if his skills were as valuable to the future of the organization as his champions had maintained, to engage in an all-out fundraising campaign to cover the costs of his return. After all, he was not asking any more from this organization than it had offered to him in 2005.

Instead, the board of directors took yet another turn and approached an organization called the Pottstown Area Industrial Development Corporation for a loan to pay the salary of the returning executive director for another six months. This loan, amounting to $40,000, was sold to the board as a quick fix and as an interest-free credit which, as matters developed, it turned out not to have been.[80] There was also no follow-up plan, no proposal or commitment that fundraising or an anonymous donor would maintain this fund. It is important to remember here that the maintenance of the executive director required $60,000 a year in salary plus an estimated 20% for the benefits package. Over the period of the contract, that would have increased the symphony's liability by approximately $280,000 above and beyond its other obligations.

However, neither the supportive board members nor the music director nor the executive director, himself, were aware of the precariousness of the

---

[79] Nonprofit Business Analysis by the Nonprofit Finance Fund, March 2008.
[80] Minutes of the Pottstown Symphony Orchestra Board of Directors' Meeting (President's Report) from April 25, 2007.

situation. There had been memos circulated within the orchestra noting that, among others, the William Penn Foundation had requested that the symphony withdraw its application for a $75,000 grant award simply because it now had no executive director. This was in late 2006 or early 2007. It is now clear from the internal memos circulating at that time that the thinking was to secure the services of the man who had made this application possible, pocket the money and let the funding for his position run out, returning thereafter to an all-volunteer structure with the possible exception of the music director. In fact, the Nonprofit Finance Fund report of March 2008 shows exactly this pattern during the years 2002, 2003, 2004 and the first half of 2005, following the firing and payment of compensatory damages to the first executive director several years before.[81]

Prior to his departure from the organization, at the end of December 2006, the now returning executive director had recognized the impact of his leaving the organization on its capacity to secure funding and had offered to act in an interim and freelance manner until the organization could engage a full-time ED. In a memo from January 8, 2007, barely a week following the ED's departure for his new position in Europe, the music director sent the following to the president, vice-president and treasurer of the organization.

"After much thought, the recent encounter with the William Penn Foundation has raised serious concerns to me as to whether or not the Pottstown Symphony Orchestra Association will actually receive the NEA grant should NEA find out you no longer have an executive director. If they ask, you cannot lie,

This indicates a leaderless ship to serious philanthropic organizations, hence WP's request that you withdraw your proposal. Please remember, neither the board nor the executive committee is viewed by comparable philanthropic organizations as the CEO, and a CEO is what big granters want to see in place.

Without an executive leader, I am also fearful you will have as much chance with other large philanthropic organizations as you recently have had with WP."[82]

The proposal of the former executive director and the recommendation to accept this proposal made by the music director were not accepted by the board officers and the further consequence of this rejection of a proposal that might have made a difference to the symphony's funding picture was

---

[81] Nonprofit Business Analysis – Pottstown Symphony. Nonprofit Finance Fund. March 2008, page 19.
[82] Memo from the Music Director of the Pottstown Symphony to the Board President, Vice-President and Treasurer dated January 8, 2007.

the request of the Philadelphia Foundation, made in early 2007, that the Pottstown Symphony withdraw its application for a grant simply because it did not have an executive head.[83] The following and sardonic comment was entered into the minutes of the board meeting reporting this development: "The board discussed this briefly."[84]

In the meantime, the suggestion of the board member who would face impeachment in several months that the orchestra launch a serious fundraising campaign and his report following his meeting with a major fundraising expert who had called attention to the successful campaign that had been conducted for the restoration of the Sunnybrook Ballroom in Pottsgrove, was met with skepticism and hesitation. "There were board hesitations which included the effort that would be involved and a feasibility/assessment survey needed."[85] From the protocol of this board meeting in April 2007, it seems that the primary discussions revolved around the PAID loan to pay for the return of the executive director, the governance committee report and matters of nomination. No time was lost to any discussion of life following the exhaustion of the PAID loan.

As would have been expected, with no fundraising and a miserable debt picture which precluded successful grants and funding applications, the remaining, available balance from the PAID loan was rapidly approaching zero. In late November, 2007, the music director again took the initiative and advised the board of its responsibility to the person whom they had re-hired less than six months ago and to the organization. There was little response but, from certain circles, both the music director and the executive director started to hear how their opinions and warnings were not wanted. The dominance mentality had taken hold here and the relationships between the staff and the board, especially those with the executive staff, had deteriorated. Any sense of trust in this board or in its ability to manage the personnel issues and other matters responsibly had been lost. By the end of 2007, the board had sunk itself deeply and dangerously in the writing and re-writing of governance rules, each of which was more draconic that the last. The board as a decision making body had all but abrogated its authority and by doing so had lost any remaining traces of respect that should have been afforded to it.

This situation festered into a series of confrontations following the impeachment of the now departed board member. In January, a senior

---

[83] Minutes of the Pottstown Symphony Orchestra Board of Directors' Meeting from April 25, 2007.
[84] Ibid.
[85] Ibid.

member of the board approached an attorney in Valley Forge, Pennsylvania, and arranged for a meeting with him to discuss a potential putsch against this now rogue board structure. His points, stated in a memo of January 1, 2008, included the impeachment action without board approval, the disastrous and long-term lack of leadership, lack of long-term solutions to chronic financial problems, the failure to treat the employees with minimal respect, and other issues which impacted on the stagnation which had overcome the organization. The attorney questioned felt this sort of action was dangerous but, to be successful, it had to be led from within the organization. He offered advice but declined to represent any minority opinion since he felt the issue of damages and litigation on the part of the deposed board members and the damage to the organization may prove to be too much and put the continued survival of the organization at risk.

In the meanwhile, the symphony had decided to reorganize its strategic planning committee and the representative of the medical products firm that had become the orchestra's season sponsor in 2007 offered to co-chair this effort. He and the executive director along with a few others knew that the real impulse of this strategic reorganization would have to be to force the symphony board to face its increasing mountain of debt. A systematic analysis was undertaken by him in the form of a questionnaire to the board. The replies showed how serious the confrontation between board and staff had become. On the one hand, the talent and creativity of the executive director and music director, their professionalism, creativity, vision and entrepreneurial thinking were praised by one segment while the other side bemoaned their alienation of community support, their negative and paranoid actions and their not being held accountable for divisive statements and actions. There were even those on the board who protested that the tension between the board and the music director and executive director was draining their enthusiasm. The point that this board had hardly showed constructive enthusiasm and initiative in its tackling of any effort, even of initiatives organized from within its own ranks, was never discussed. The initial *faux pas* of not including the music director in this process that would decide the orchestra's future direction and have a profound impact on the course of the symphony for years to come, may have been a simple oversight. It was not to be expected that the man from the medical systems company would have understood the impact of the conductor on this process. However, others on the board would or should have done so. Eventually, following a memo sent by the executive director to this committee complaining: "A major factor in the strategic plan and one of the two most significant line items on the budget is the artistic side. For us to have a meeting, at least initially, and to do so without the input of the music director seems to me to be, somehow, wrong."[86] The committee relented and the music director was invited to participate.

Another yet typical example of this lack of enthusiasm for the board's own projects occurred in early 2006. The member of the board who had garnered his seat there by donating $1,000 to the former president presented to the board the idea that they should host a show house in Pottstown for a month. His projections, based on such successful exhibits in affluent and historically rich communities in the northeastern USA, showed that the symphony stood to profit grandly from opening a historic home to visitors for a period of 30 days. However well-meaning this project may have been it quickly became evident that, in fact, there had been little research into its dangers and no preparation for the administrative burden it would cause. The then sitting board president pressured the executive director for his support for the project. It was clear to the executive director that this would prove to be nothing less than a financial debacle for the symphony. He did assist in the preparation of a realistic budget and began researching the personnel and other needs such a project would have. Meanwhile, the initiator of the scheme did little but promise contracts to certain vendors even though the project had not been approved and no money for it had been allocated. The executive director's position was that this was presented as a board project by a board member and it was the responsibility of the board and the project director to organize this initiative. First the board president all but commanded him to take over this behemoth of an initiative which was to be carried out at a time when the symphony was seriously understaffed and no one on the board was interested in lending the time, money or effort to realize such a task. The excuse was that this board member was an "idea man", a somewhat lame excuse for passing the buck onto the staff and letting the board or the then president either garner the gains from a successful realization or giving her a scapegoat if, as projected, the plan fell apart.

The then orchestra manager belonged to the same circle of church goers as did the board president and her circle on the board. He sent an email to the executive director in which he was critical that the executive director refused to stand behind this project. No doubt, he was put up to this action since it was clear in his text that he had simply re-quoted the statements of the board president, uttered in a meeting several days before. Typical for him and for the Pottstown Symphony, however, was the failure to do his or its homework. The board had not understood that such projects require close to a year to organize, require effective and serious marketing, require a full-

---

[86] Memo from Executive Director to Strategic Planning Committee dated February 25, 2008.

time project head and that they often come with start-up costs of up to $25,000 and more. In June 2006, the Pottstown Symphony had no cash reserves not to speak of the potential $25,000 it would need to make this work. The fundraiser from the nearby Phoenixville Y.M.C.A. had confirmed these start-up costs to the executive director during a meeting of the Montgomery County Foundation in Norristown just a few days earlier. He had been involved in such show-house projects, himself, and had acquired first-hand experience into the labor-intensive structuring of such an initiative. The factor that Pottstown, itself, despite several Victorian homes was rapidly going downhill and had become little more than a drug, prostitution and poverty center, was given no notice. In his reply to the orchestra manager, the executive director had just come away from another unsavory experience with another member of this board. He had been frontally attacked, as was Porter Eidam almost 10 years before, simply because the massive amounts of fundraising he had undertaken didn't produce results fast enough for this one board member, the daughter of the presumed founder of the orchestra and music teacher at a local school. She had done nothing at all to assist in fundraising for the organization and, herself, had little interest in the mechanisms through which one secures funding, but this presumed birthright she carried and her holding a seat on this board gave her authority to initiate a frontal attack on someone she and the board president simply didn't like. The executive director wrote the following in his reply to the orchestra manager: "…It makes me angry that I'm breaking my ass trying to raise money and someone like a certain board member last night criticizes me because the funds don't flow in fast enough for her. Do you know…that since October, I've written over $1,000,000 in grant applications? I'm sick and tired of being criticized for working my ass off."[87]

However, this singular attack on the executive director and that on Porter Eidam almost 10 years before were no isolated incidents. The music director was a regular target of these rabid outbursts coming from the then seated board president, from the board member cited above and, later, from the newly elected vice-president who had written his memo to the executive director in late 2005 as follow-up to the broadside sent by the then president. Later, the newly acquired Business on Board candidate joined this sport and lost no occasion to fire volleys at the music director.

The high-point in these volleys, however, was reached in the summer 2006 at the point when the superintendent of schools was to finally step down from her 20 year reign at the head of the board of directors. She was replaced by

---

[87] Memo from Executive Director to Orchestra Manager from June 22, 2006.

an inept and weak successor, the wife of the aforementioned headmaster, who initially believed everything said to her by her predecessor. In Pottstown, relationships were always more important that facts or competence. Believing the word of her "friend" and former board president, she assigned to the newly elected vice-president the task of carrying on a personnel evaluation of the music director. This was to be done via a survey sent to the entire orchestra where the musicians could rate her performance. The tale was told that this was usual practice, which it was not, and that in Pottstown this was done all the time, which was also untrue. The newly elected vice-president was anxious to show his authority and, as a follower of the departing board president, was already convinced that the music director had to be forced out. Using his own stationery and his home address and not going through channels in the organization, he conducted a secretive evaluation by sending to each and every musician a multi-page questionnaire with which to rate the music director. Many of the questions touched on issues of "democratic" management of the orchestra and "time for personal discussions between the music director and the musicians regarding artistic decisions", matters which are solely within the authority of the music director who, by nature of this role as artistic leader, assumes absolute authority over what goes on in the orchestra while conducting concerts or rehearsals. This must be so for such a diversified structure to operate at all. Furthermore, these surveys did not take into account that the orchestra was a per-service ensemble and that, aside from a small core of regulars who would perform the majority of the concerts, the personnel would be different from performance to performance. Added to this was the fact that many who had received this survey had not performed with the Pottstown Symphony for many years and a few had only worked once or twice under this music director. For these musicians, any fair evaluation would be all but impossible but, for many, this didn't stop them from completing and returning the evaluation questionnaire anyway.

Worst of all, however, was the simple fact that this newly-elected vice-president introduced himself as VP of the Pottstown Symphony at a time when he still had no authority within the organization and was days away from assuming the newly-elected role of vice-president. When this survey was sent, he was nothing but a regular board member. It is clear that this action was initiated by the outgoing board president who, in a board retreat, would later make it clear that the music director and executive director were at the root of the problems in the symphony and that something had to be done about them now!

Both the orchestra's personnel contractor and the executive director signaled alarm at this action, first to the music director and, shortly thereafter, to the newly elected president of the board who did nothing to address the growing problem surrounding this music director survey. This was to become the modus operandi for her entire tenure and her failure to act or her incorrect actions would accelerate the revolution going on within the organization and would lead to its ceasing to function in any form. There were many emails to the new president from the executive director, each one more earnest than the former and each one increasingly alerting the new board president that through this rogue action she was risking litigation from the music director. It was finally through an action; initiated by the music director through her attorney, that this farce was stopped in its tracks but not before the damage had been done to the orchestra, to the integrity of the board and to the already crippled relationships between the board and the executive team.

However, such behavior was not restricted to board – staff relationships alone. The attacks on certain board members by other, more aggressive ones such as the man from Business on Board destroyed whatever may have been left of a respectful and professional style. The sentence in the impeachment memo of September 2007, "…by these actions…you harmfully undermine the work that this board has undertaken to satisfy the mission of the association"[88] had now been turned around and by virtue of attacks by certain board members, many of whom were also part of the impeachment procedure, the organization reverted into chaos.

The new board president tried to smooth out these rough edges in board behavior, not with a firm hand and fair and creative policies and a focus, but by organizing periodic board retreats to discuss the challenges and solutions facing the organization. The first of these, led by the executive director of the Harrisburg Symphony Orchestra, was well presented and addressed many of the core matters troubling the organization such as the stewardship responsibilities of the board, the leadership of the executive director, the importance of retaining a quality music director and general issues regarding direction, strategic planning and marketing and public outreach. This occurred in late 2006. By 2007, these board retreats had deteriorated into secret conclaves where the executive team was not allowed to participate and where the leader of the retreat would have the attendees spend hours piecing together paper airplanes from scrap as a way to show their ability to work together. It was at one of these, later retreats, that the earlier board president demanded something be done against the music director and executive director since they were at the core of the orchestra's problems.

---

[88] Impeachment Defense Response to Filed Grievance. Memo of the Vice-President of the PSOA from 28 September 2007.

In fact, it was not the insistence of the executive employees that the board fundraise and that their livelihoods be secured that was the only problem with this organization. It must be stated that even certain benefits which were contractual commitments made by the board to the employees at the time of hiring were simply cancelled by the board when it began to run out of money but that the effected employee was never informed of the cancellation, either before the fact nor thereafter. As has been previously told here, it remained to the executive director to discover this fact when he requested a new medical ID, months after his re-hire.

What seems to have been wrong with this board of directors was its inability to self-evaluate, to view itself critically; to adopt a system whereby it would judge itself on its actions and on the results those actions brought. Instead, the philosophy of the board member from Business on Board, a person who had no business, whatsoever, belonging to the board of a cultural non-profit organization and who had neither interest in or knowledge of classical music, sadly betrays the attitude of self-defense that ruled the organization after July 2007. In several meetings, most notably in a strategic planning meeting to which he had been invited, he bullied the host and chairman of the meeting, the internal auditor of the medical products company, hammering on the desk, raising his voice and yelling that strategic planning and fund raising are all nonsense. The first thing the Pottstown Symphony needs is governance. That was the problem. In 2005, as the Pottstown Symphony approached the then American Symphony Orchestra League for advice, it had gotten it right. The bad advice from the League that they needed an executive director instead of the planned business manager and fundraiser set the orchestra on a collision course with its own past. The board was ruled by a president who could not and would not give up authority to an experienced and qualified executive director, partially because she was ignorant of her function but mostly because her raison d'être was to retain her hold on power and the internal friction grew until the wheels of the organization began to squeak and stresses on its structure led to a complete and irreversible breakdown.

Had the board sat back and asked itself a few simple questions such as what it was ready to relinquish in authority and what needs did it really expect to see fulfilled from assuming a professional structure, none of this story would have happened and the Pottstown Symphony Orchestra could be in existence today instead of defunct and relegated to some sort of quasi-legal limbo with the Damocles sword of litigation hanging over its head yet another time.

5. BOARD MEMBER LOANS

The Financial Side

"In 1992, when the American Symphony Orchestra League published a benchmark study of the financial condition of symphony orchestras,[89] the prediction was that by the year 2000, the orchestra industry and individual orchestras would be in financial crisis if they did not significantly change the way they did business. Subsequently, the United States experienced one of the most vigorous and sustained economic booms in its history...Many misread the trends as harbingers of a new economic order leading to unending vistas of permanent prosperity. Orchestras for the most part did not heed the warnings of the 1992 report."[90]

Superficially, however, the demographic profile of Pottstown, Pennsylvania may have had the general stability the community would have needed to have supported and maintained a small local or amateur orchestra but not an ensemble with stated aims to become a regional or widely known one. In 2009, the estimated population of Pottstown, encompassing the zip codes 19464 and 19465 was 44,056 in 19464, which reflected an increase in that zip code of 2.4% over the previous census taken in the year 2000. This same census showed a population of 13,700 in zip code 19465. However, Pottstown is a divided community, and these two zip codes betray strikingly different demographic profiles. The zip code 19465 is in the more affluent Chester County with a median resident age approaching 40 years old and with approximately 40% of its population engaged in professional or managerial employment. Additionally, 56.7% of this work force in this zip code earns a household income of more than $50,000 a year. 75.8% of these citizens in 19465 are home owners as opposed to only 63% in zip code 19464, the poorer half of Pottstown where the estimated per capita income was only $20,923. Also, it must not be forgotten that the 19464 half of Pottstown, including the outlying regions of Sanatoga and Pottsgrove, has a population of over 44,000 while 19465 has only 16,200 residents and that in 19464, the poorer portion of Pottstown, the core population of Pottstown Borough amounts to only about 20,000 people. Also a factor in this mix is the fact that 40% of the 19465 population works in managerial or professional employment as opposed to only 28.5% of those living in 19464.

---

[89] The Wolf Organization, Inc.: *The Financial Condition of Symphony Orchestras.* (Washington, DC: American Symphony Orchestra League, 1992).
[90] Dr. Thomas Wolf & Nancy Glaze: *And the Band Stopped Playing – The Rise and Fall of the San Jose Symphony.* (Cambridge, MA, Wolf, Keens & Company, 2005), page 52.

In the year 2010, the City-Data.com crime index for 19464 was 539 with the US national average hovering around 319.1.[91]

The United States Department of Labor qualifies the poverty line in the USA as an income of less than $13,130 for a family of two. In the year 2010, in Pottstown as a whole, 11.3% of the population lived with incomes below that minimum.

For a symphony orchestra a deeper look into this profile shows an inordinate risk for the organization were it to try and maintain itself as a Pottstown based ensemble and seek to secure its funding and support from within the borders of the community and its immediate suburbs. Although the regional unemployment figures for 2012 were significantly below the national average (4.63% for 19464 and 2.56% for 19465), a large number of those living in 19464 were earning only marginal incomes. It is exactly this group that is not and cannot be expected to show much interest in sustaining a symphony orchestra in the community. Reflecting on the educational levels in this region encompassing zip code 19464, only 37% of the population has earned a high school diploma. This is a strong contrast to the statistics in 19465 which show that 89.1% of the population claims a high school diploma or better with a mere 11% only having completed elementary school or some high school. In real numbers this means that of the 16,237 residents in 19465, only about 1,800 have not yet achieved an educational level where the arts and culture generally play an important role in their lives. In 19464, however, this number increases to over 13,000 based on the Pottstown borough-only population of about 22,000 persons.[92]

The realization that this level of poverty and with an educational standard that, in contrast to a major city or, in fact, to Silicon Valley in California where almost half of the work force has, at least, to some degree, a college or university education and some exposure to arts and culture in its environs, Pottstown was sorely lacking in this basic exposure to the arts that would create even a marginally loyal audience, even at a purely grassroots level.[93]

It was necessary for the Pottstown Symphony, were it to survive in this environment, to look towards expanding itself outside of its immediate region. When the San José Symphony in California closed its doors in 2002, the reasons for this decline were a fatal mixture of staff and board errors and an inability to see the warning signs pointing to a too rapid expansion of the orchestra's horizons. The San José Symphony flourished for almost 125 years in an environment which provided room and audiences for up to 28

---

[91] www.city-data.com/zips/19464.html and www.city-data.com/zips/19465.html.
[92] http://www.city-data.com/city/Pottstown-Pennsylvania.html.
[93] http://www.city-data.com/city/San-Jose-California.html.

symphony orchestras, 4 opera companies, 9 choral groups, 10 performing arts series and 3 classical music festivals.[94] The Pottstown Symphony, however, entered the year 2000 in an environment where only three professional orchestras and seven community orchestras were active. One of these professional orchestras was the Pottstown Symphony itself. In addition, both the well-established Reading Symphony (16 miles to the west) and the Philadelphia Orchestra (40 miles to the east) provided competition for the ensemble. Aside from several other and less important ensembles scattered throughout the region, the period from 2000 until 2006 or 2008 should have been the golden age of the Pottstown Symphony with its quantum increase in its artistic and musical level, the competence of its conductor, especially after 2002, and the increasing attention it was receiving from both the press outside of Pottstown and, after 2006, also from classical record labels. However, what proved the undoing of the Pottstown Symphony was its simple refusal of the board which had recommended and approved this expansion to recognize the financial and administrative burden such an expansion would and must put on the board and on the orchestra. Perhaps it might have been better for the symphony or, perhaps more honest of its board, to have decided in 2002 to return the symphony to its initial status as a community orchestra. Whether the decision to shoot for the heavens was the result of excessive ambition or simply a matter of false evaluation of the responsibilities this move would mean for the symphony is something one cannot properly judge from this distance. However, the result of this action shows that by taking it without proper consideration of its meaning, the board of the Pottstown Symphony made its greatest and most fatal judgmental error.

As early as the 2004-2005 fiscal year, the financial picture of the Pottstown Symphony had begun to show cracks. Although in 2003, the annual budget showed a cash shortfall of $6,340 by 2004-2005 this amount had increased to an estimated deficit of $64,241 based on seasonal expenses amounting to $294,546. Of course the engagement of the new music director as a full-time employee in 2005 did increase the costs to the symphony but that only amounted to about $30,000 of the total since, for much of the period from 2002 until 2005 she had been working as a free-lance employee, without any benefits package and, after 2005, the cost of her full-time employment was to be covered by the promised "Mr. X Fund". Where this analysis is faulty, however, lies in the overzealous assignment of expected donations to the orchestra budget. Organizations that had contributed on a one-time basis in

---

[94] Dr. Thomas Wolf & Nancy Glaze: *And the Band Stopped Playing – The Rise and Fall of the San Jose Symphony. (Cambridge, MA, Wolf, Keens & Company, 2005)* , p. 85.

2003 were automatically added to the 2004-2005 budget as if it was expected that they would donate again, which they did not. This naïve misrepresentation of the situation amounted to a false estimate which was almost $13,000 above what could have been reasonably anticipated to have been donated to the symphony. In addition, the loans picture within the organization was misrepresented or, better stated, not represented at all. In addition to an outstanding loan amounting to $52,000 which had been granted by the local Harleysville National Bank there was also the outstanding sum of $19,000 which had been loaned to the ensemble by the orchestra manager and an open line of credit amounting to an additional $10,000. In its 2005 tax return, the Pottstown Symphony Orchestra Association states in its form I-990 that it carried at that time liabilities of $19,000 (Part IV, Line 63) and $62,322 (Part IV, Line 64)[95]

Particularly onerous is the $19,000 loan from the then orchestra manager. Apart from the consideration that an employee should not have been expected to lend this amount, or, in fact, any amount to his employer since the acquisition of necessary funding is the responsibility of the board in fulfillment of its stewardship function, the terms under which this loan was granted seemingly betray a developing uncertainty on the part of the creditor. This loan for $19,000 was granted in two installments, in April 2005 for a $12,000 and in May 2005 for an additional $7,000 principal plus interest on a sliding scale that began at 6% in May 2005 and increased to 8% in June 2006. This meant the amount to be repaid would, upon maturity, have amounted to $20,068.43 but the creditor agreed to donate the interest payments back to the orchestra if the note was satisfied before the end of June 2006. This did not occur. Instead, this loan was to later become a contentious issue which would put further strain on both the organization and its employees and lead to a destructive tug-of-war and a catastrophic breach of faith and trust among the then orchestra manager, the executive team and the symphony.

Up until October, 2005, the Pottstown Symphony Orchestra Association had entrusted its fundraising to the hands of a board member who was also a member of the orchestra. It is important to remember that this board member straddled the roles of management and employee in her position as a tenured cellist with the symphony. More will be said about this person later in this narrative but, for now, it must be emphasized that she seemed to have viewed her fundraising activities for the symphony as a territorial imperative. The fact that she was paid a commission based on the amounts

---

[95] Return of Organization Exempt from Income Tax, IRS Form I-990 for the tax year beginning July 1, 2005. Source: GuideStar.org.

she secured from foundation and governmental grants poses, at the very least, an ethical concern. However, the arrival of a new executive director, in October 2005, with the responsibility to fund-raise for the organization, should have compelled her to share the information she had with him. Instead, this territorialism resulted in months where the information flow between the executive director and the now, former fund raiser and still board member was de facto non-existent. In December 2005, the music director wrote to the then president of the board and to the orchestra manager: "It is up to the board to inform [our fundraising board member] that she must communicate not only with the music director and outside involved persons re: grant specs, but she must also communicate with the orchestra manager, especially if the grant involves specific orchestra operations issues. Communication is [her] biggest downfall as a grant writer. If this problem is not addressed by the board ASAP, the PSO will feel the effects monetarily…It is also up to the board to make it very clear to her that when the executive director asks 1) to meet with her and 2) to forward copies of all recent PSO grant applications, which she has submitted over the past season, that these requests are being made because 1) it is HIS JOB to seek out new and connect with previous financial resources and 2) it is now HIS JOB to write the grants that will enable the PSO to continue to exist. It is my understanding that, to date, neither of the aforementioned has occurred."[96]

Aside from the proprietary nature of this board member's behavior, there existed the undeniable fact, expressed by the music director to the executive director, that the board president and her personnel officer had no wish to engage him into this position. In a memo written by the personnel officer to the board president and music director and dated 19 April 2005, she commented: "We have received over 15 responses to the job posting, with most of them coming from CareerBuilder. There are probably six that have some promise particularly with background and salary requirements. All of the six are from the Delaware Valley."[97] It was clear from this report and the nature of this selection that the personnel officer was not at all interested in hiring anyone from outside the region but, instead, restricted her narrowing-down of the candidates to only those from within the local area. Additionally, no one can know how many additional applications may have resulted from the job having been posted on the League of American Orchestras' employment pages. CareerBuilder is not a specialist site for arts

---

[96] Memo from Music Director to PSOA Board President and Pottstown Symphony Orchestra Association Orchestra Manager from 07 December 2005.
[97] Memo from Personnel Director to Board President and Music Director from 19 April 2005.

management executives but the applicants from the League site would have also been orchestra professionals. Presumably the placement among the then ASOL on-line job placements was nothing more than a shallow concession to presumed professionalism and to the "League" of which the Pottstown Symphony was a member orchestra. In any case, this "League" placement service was free to all its institutional members. It may also have been the case that the then human resources board member was simply uncomfortable with evaluating resumes coming from experienced or simply well-trained professionals in the field. However, it was even at this level that the aforementioned board xenophobia became visible. Regardless of qualifications, a candidate from outside of the immediate Pottstown region had little chance here. It was due to the intervention and protests of the music director, who accidently gained access to the executive director's resume and application which had come to the symphony through the ASOL web site, that he became a candidate at all for the job.

However, candidacy in the usual sense did not necessarily denote acceptance. Following each interview, the soon-to-become executive director was generally branded as "chauvinistic" because he directed answers to questions regarding orchestra management to the music director, the orchestra manager or the personnel contractor for the ensemble, in short to the professionals in the organization and not to the board president. It went overlooked in this criticism that the music director was also a woman. Once hired, he was still disliked by the board president and her circle. In a last-ditch move to keep him from starting the position, the board president delayed for a period of weeks putting her signature to an important letter requested by the Immigration and Naturalization Service of the US Government which would confirm his employment so his wife in Germany could be issued her Immigrant Visa or "Green Card". It was only through an active intervention of the music director who forced this signature and expressed the needed letter to the new executive director in Germany, a letter that had previously been drafted by the incoming executive director himself and presented to the board president for transfer to symphony stationery and her signature, that the "Green Card" application was not delayed. The strong suspicion exists that, having failed on all fronts to get rid of the unwanted executive director, the board president used her "friendship" with "Mr. X" to insure the drying up of the special fund. What enforces this suspicion is a statement made to the executive director by the symphony's attorney in December, 2006: "She doesn't like you." That was her style with anyone she didn't like, either in the Pottstown Symphony (see the circumstances surrounding the dismissal of the first executive director), or in her job as school superintendent.

Already, in April 2005, others on the board were beginning to express their concerns about the growing debt picture. In April, 2005, months before the arrival of the new executive director and during the period where the search for candidates for this position was in full swing, the then treasurer of the Pottstown Symphony and a vice-president of one of the local banks wrote the following: "Fundraising – I was going to impress once again upon EVERYONE the need to generate gifts, grants, contributions, donations for the remainder of THIS season."[98] The words capitalized in this sentence were done so by the author of the memo. Although himself not an especially active fund raiser, he did watch over a $10,000 annual donation his bank made to the symphony and, as a member of the board and an officer of this bank, he was, at least, aware of the seriousness of a rapidly worsening problem.

The uncommunicative grant writer, board member and musician had attempted to make inroads to the prestigious William Penn Foundation in Philadelphia but had been refused since, simply enough; the foundation knew of the orchestra but had had no opportunity to hear it in performance. This had been a long-standing criteria established by the William Penn Foundation prior to inviting an organization to submit a proposal. Evidently, in submitting this inquiry at what seems to have been rather late in the ongoing season, this factor was disregarded by her.

As the financial problems within the ensemble increased and the debt climbed, there was, once again, a plea from the treasurer and banker and representative of a major donor for some action at the board level. In a memo dated 17 March 2006 he wrote the following, addressed to all members of the board: "I admit to more than a little frustration. We spent a large part of last Monday's meeting discussing the current cash flow crunch and financial situation of the PSO. The strategic planning committee by-passed their regular agenda in March and spent several hours developing a list of potential donors. That list was circulated at the board meeting and members were asked to select one or two names to contact…Attached is the updated list of those who have volunteered to contact the businesses/individuals. What is all too readily apparent are the board members whose names are not on the list."[99]

Increasingly, the seriousness of the financial shortcomings the symphony faced began to be reflected in the slowness with which employees were

---

[98] Memo from Treasurer of the Pottstown Symphony Orchestra Association to Board President, Personnel Manager and Music Director from 20 April 2005.
[99] Memo from Treasurer of the Pottstown Symphony Orchestra Association to all board members from 17 March 2006.

reimbursed for approved and valid travel and expenses. At about this time (mid 2006), the music director began to make known the amounts owed to her by the board and the association and included them in her monthly report to the board which would then become a matter of public record as part of the minutes of those meetings. In 2007, the executive committee's response to this seeming affront from the music director was to refuse to include either the music director or executive director reports in the minutes of the board meetings. It was not that these reports were overly long. In general, they were only bullet points. What seemed to have irked these people was the consistent and correct inclusion by the music director of the amounts due to her in each of her monthly reports as well as the need to still the impression, contained in these reports, that the music director and executive director were actively working in the interests of the orchestra while the board sat back and idly watched these initiatives, contributing little or nothing to them. At the same time, special initiatives by both the music director and executive director to save the symphony money or, in one case, to both save money and raise funds through cooperation with a travel agency, were disregarded by the board. In this one case, an agreement was made with a regional travel agency who was also in partnership with the firm, Collette Vacations. Collette had initiated a tour package for Europe entitled "Mozart's Musical Cities" where symphony orchestras had profited through selling passage on this tour through cities in Austria and the Czech Republic, sometimes also accompanied by the participating orchestra's music director as narrator. The tour included not only the sightseeing portion but also concerts and bits of history about Mozart and his contemporaries told in the places where he had lived and worked. In June, 2006 both the music director and executive director had informed the board of a presentation to be given by the travel agency and Collette Vacations. Already, the travel agency had promised to the orchestra its help with free flights from Europe for one or more of the Pottstown Symphony's upcoming soloists. In addition, the estimated profits to the symphony from a successful tour and a minimum of 20 bookings would have been a great help in the increasingly urgent need to satisfy the bottom line.

Initially, although Collette Vacations is an internationally operating and highly respected travel company which had previously worked with other orchestras in the region, each of whom had produced respectable fundraising numbers through their participation in just such an offer, the board of the Pottstown Symphony stood prepared to reject the idea. It is difficult to understand whether the motivation was simple disinterest, the feeling that participation would be expected from board members or a general disregard of ideas coming from the staff. In any case, it was demanded of the executive director that he secure copious references for Collette Vacations, which he did, and only reluctantly did the board approve this plan. The date of the showcase was announced to the board and all were urged to participate. This was the key launch event for this action and the music director, executive director, a representative of Collette Vacations and the owner of the travel agency, a company from Wyomissing, Pennsylvania, were to attend and to make the presentation and initial sales. It would have been imperative for the board to, at least, show its solidarity by being present in the room or by sending one or more representatives. In fact, not a single person from the board, not an officer or the banker who often went on such tours and cruises with his wife, nor any of the school teachers with an obvious and vested interest in the educational content of such a tour, either showed up at this event nor expressed any interest in it at all. The usual excuse was that they had already made vacation plans which, be that true or not, was something that had developed after this fundraising initiative had been announced at a board meeting several months before. Complaints from the travel agency and from the music director and executive director that a board presence would have given the needed support and credibility to this action went unheeded and not one single member of the board either signed on himself or exerted an effort to sell the package to friends and associates. For lack of interest, the required minimal number of participants for the tour was never reached and the trip was cancelled and, with it, any future expectations the Pottstown Symphony may have had for assistance in its travel requirements from the Wyomissing travel agency. This lethargy cost the symphony bitterly and resulted in increased costs which, with little minimal effort from the board, could have been avoided.

By the end of 2007, the Pottstown Symphony Orchestra's tax returns showed a dangerous level of debt and obligations which, without dramatic action from the board, could never have been satisfied. In the I-990 from the 2006-2007 fiscal year, the obligations of the symphony to outside lenders consisted of the $19,000 owed the orchestra manager, a $21,850 loan made by the former treasurer, a $20,000 loan made by the new vice-president, a $1,500 loan made by another board member, the $9,950 still due on the symphony's line of credit and a $48,713 balance on the original $50k loan made by the Harleysville Bank. This was a total indebtedness of $121,013. Added to this was the $40,000 loan made to the symphony earlier that year to assure the salary for the now rehired executive director who was to return in July, 2007. With the burden of salary and benefits the rehired executive director would bring when he would return in July, the Pottstown Symphony Orchestra Association was facing the repayment of over $160,000 in debt and, already, the Harleysville Bank was deciding to cancel the symphony's line of credit, even if it managed to repay the principal due. It is in this same tax return that the symphony made it known that its income from concerts and other activities was only $47,841.

The executive director had begun to warn the board, sometime in the autumn of 2007, that it looked like the USA was about to enter into a significant recession. The economic prognoses to be read in both the Wall Street Journal and major newspapers and magazines as well other financial reports signaled an impending economic decline. Not being a financial expert, the executive director could not have predicted the depth of the recession of 2008 and the fatal consequences this would have for arts organizations as well as for the general public. Clearly, what happened in 2008 was not merely a recession but approached the levels of the Great Depression of 1929. Still, an organization like the Pottstown Symphony, had it heeded the warnings, could have downsized and passionately fundraised and survived on low flame until the crisis was over. Instead, both bankers on the board discounted the advice and warnings of the executive director and maintained that boom times would continue indefinitely. There was still little fundraising carried on except for a community action at Friendly's Family Restaurant in Pottstown, from time to time, where the board played waitress and the symphony could keep the tips, a few half-hearted attempts at motivating personal fundraising contacts, and an occasional church-based or other action which was more of a social nature than it was true fundraising. At this stage, the level of debt carried by the symphony was so dramatic that granting organizations and major foundations increasingly refused to support the orchestra.

In January, 2007, the crisis had peaked to where a business leader, owner of a major audio post-production firm in Philadelphia and a member of the board who had been active in scolding this group for its failure to act responsibly, proposed that the current season be cancelled and the association consider initiating bankruptcy proceedings. As a response, the music director proposed making dramatic cuts which, had they been taken, would have saved face but little else. Her interest was in preserving the integrity of the organization but she was correct in her view that the current impasse was something that could be quickly overcome given some effort on the part of the board. In her memo of 25 January 2007, she wrote the following: "If orchestras with multi-million dollar budgets can raise $1.5 million dollars in REAL CASH, not pledges, in 30 days, it is my opinion if approached aggressively the Association could raise $250K in REAL CASH, not pledges, in 30 days. But you will have to ACT."[100]

---

[100] Memo from Music Director to the Board of Directors dated 25 January 2007.

The board member who had made the proposal to shut down the current season replied: "For some reason no one wanted to talk to me after the meeting! Nonetheless, I feel the mission accomplished – they all woke up. We can't guarantee they won't go to bed again, but at least they didn't put it off for another month. There's an "emergency" board meeting scheduled for next Wednesday. [The symphony's attorney] should be there...I hope something happens soon. There's only so much time I can put into something that doesn't bear fruit."[101]

It didn't take long before word started to get around that the Pottstown Symphony had, at least superficially, begun to realize that it was in genuine trouble. Remembering the board member who was also the fundraiser and a musician in the orchestra, it becomes obvious that her tripartite role in this drama may have motivated her to also assume the role of mole for the musicians' union. Certainly the actions and decisions taken in a board meeting should have been held confidential and sacred by the members of the board, regardless of the subsidiary roles a board member may have played. It is also possible that the daughter of the presumed founder of the Pottstown Symphony, a woman who had, by this time, left the board and had become an enemy of the hired management team, passed confidential information on to the union via the former board president who, at this point, still held a board seat but not with the status of an officer. In any case, the new board president received a letter from the Secretary of Local 135-211 of the American Federation of Musicians which began as follows: "We have learned of the substantial debt incurred by the Pottstown Symphony Orchestra as well as a proposal to consider declaring bankruptcy that was discussed last Wednesday evening by PSO board members."[102] It is astounding how swiftly this piece of news had managed to travel from Pottstown to Reading, Pennsylvania. It is clear from the content of this letter that the privileged communications shared at board meetings were of no importance when there was a different political motivation at stake. Also, the conclusions drawn by the Reading local in this letter show a schizophrenic understanding of the seriousness of the Pottstown Symphony Orchestra's financial misery. On one hand, the union proposed: "...that the PSO escrow the musician's payroll for the remaining concerts of the 2006/07 season...I realize that such a proposal can seem unusual. In view of the extraordinary events that have transpired over the course of recent months, however, along with the growing awareness among PSO members that the orchestra is currently facing unusual financial challenges, an escrow practice makes a lot

---

[101] Ibid.
[102] Letter from the Secretary of AFM Local 135-211 (Reading, PA) to the President of the Pottstown Symphony Orchestra Association dated 12 February 2007.

of sense"[103] On the other hand, less than a year later and falling within the time frame outlined in this escrow proposal, it forced the orchestra into a collective bargaining agreement action that would only worsen the institution's precarious hold on life.

In a later chapter, we will discuss the relationships of the symphony, its musicians and its board, to the union and how this very breakdown in the integrity of the board and the violation of confidences helped lead to the failure of the orchestra to properly function as a cultural institution.

At this point in our narrative, it is important to recall the issues surrounding the impeachment procedure levied against a fellow board member as described in chapter four of this book. You will recall that the reasons given for that impeachment action, one which eventually led to the resignation of the affected board member, were his presumed "harmful and offensive behavior toward other board members, showing a malevolent attitude that is considered injurious to the morale and mission of the association."[104] In the case of the board member or members who leaked such sensitive financial information regarding a potential bankruptcy of the orchestra to the American Federation of Musicians these criteria for impeachment were not only met but exceeded. This betrayal of the trust and the confidentiality of privileged information could easily have led to the forced dissolution of the organization under pressure from the labor union. It was possible that the AFM could have imposed a boycott on the orchestra, citing its serious financial condition and growing insolvency, and advised the member musicians not to accept work with the ensemble. It must be remembered that in early 2007 the world financial crisis had not yet blossomed and the employment of free-lance musicians in the greater Philadelphia area operated at relatively normal levels. There were and would always be those with difficulty securing orchestral or ensemble work but this situation was not the norm. A draconian decision taken by the musicians' union could have meant the reversal of the symphony to its origins as an amateur orchestra.

Perhaps this potential development crossed the minds of the board and board president and of those who retained their loyalty to the former board president and her coterie but no one can know at this distance. In any case, there was no recorded mention made of this breach of trust and no disciplinary action taken against the person or persons who leaked this information. It was clear that a double standard regulating deportment and

---

[103] Ibid.
[104] Impeachment Defense Response to Filed Grievance. Memo of the Vice-President of the PSOA from 28 September 2007.

the role of a board member had become the norm at the Pottstown Symphony. A responsible board president, acting in the interests of the organization, should have immediately taken steps to discover who was acting as the mole within the Pottstown Symphony and should have immediately made motions to have this person excluded from any further participation on the board or role in the decisions taken in the name of the organization. Instead, nothing was done which begs the question as to whether the board president could have also been party to this intrigue. However, I have my own opinion regarding the identity of this person. As late as summer 2007 this individual would continue to be the leak to the union, this time with respect to a collective bargaining action. She was never disciplined. It seemed quite normal to the board and its officers that an individual could enjoy a board seat on one day and report back to the labor organization with which it was contesting a potentially expensive contract negotiation on the next. This was pure hypocrisy on the part of the president, the officers and, yes, of the executive committee that had initiated the impeachment committee initiative against a contributing and energetic and loyal member simply because he expressed his opinions to the two top employees on the management ladder. I find no excuse for this. As reader of this tale, you may decide otherwise. However, I must argue that the minimal requirement regulating the fair and equal treatment of all members of such an institution as the Pottstown Symphony is a mandate that was violated both in the case of the impeachment and in the non-action with regard to the leaking of important and sensitive information. The reasons for this double standard seem to lie in the continuing understanding of the board as a selective and restrictive club. After all, the period that lapsed between this incident in February 2007 and the impeachment proceedings against the unpopular board member was slightly longer than six months. The continuing battle between those chosen from within the social ranks of the old guard and those who came from the outside, mostly from the business world or from sponsoring organizations, was fast approaching its zenith. At all costs, the loyalty had to be maintained towards those who slavishly adhered to the traditional image of the Pottstown Symphony as a local organization only to be governed by locals who were committed to preserving this image. Disregarding the consequences this misplaced loyalty to a long dead tradition would have had, in their view, dire consequences for the orchestra. Governance was used as a pseudonym for preserving this double standard and as a vehicle with which to remove those who threatened the continuum of the Pottstown Symphony's subjectivity.

The Pottstown Symphony was in the midst of a period where it had lost its executive director and, despite warnings this could have a negative and lasting impact on any funding actions, had decided to go it alone without an executive leader. Little by little the foolishness of this decision taken by the board and its officers became known to the organization. In January 2007, an application submitted in 2006 by the music director and executive director for major funding from the William Penn Foundation in Philadelphia was rejected simply because the organization no longer had an executive director. Similarly a grant submitted to the Philadelphia Foundation which would enable the symphony to engage a professional grant writer was rejected for the same reason. The warnings expressed by the now departed executive director that by refusing to accept his offer to act as the orchestra's temporary executive head until a permanent replacement could be hired they were putting the financial future of the organization at risk had finally come home to roost and the board officers were in a quandary as to how they should react to this self-made problem. When, in March 2007, the former executive director made it known to friends in Pottstown that he would consider returning under certain predetermined circumstances which would also include his being appointed chief executive officer of the organization, the board suddenly became active. However, this activity was on nothing less than a superficial level.

At the end of April, 2007, the then treasurer distributed a revision of the Pottstown Symphony's business plan to the board. Key in this revised business plan was the acknowledgement of several, long proven, textbook truths of non-profit management. In this draft, the authors acknowledged the responsibility of the members of the board to "give, get, or go", the principle that the move towards creation of a professional orchestra required a "stronger business protocol", the reduction of the symphony's debt "in a timely fashion…working on a plan for regular repayment of monies owed, with a repayment goal of 10% each quarter", and the recognition that under the previous and now once again available executive director, "the PSOA has made customer service and attention to patron needs a hallmark of its outreach to the public."[105] The lie in this revelatory document was to be found in the rationale for its existence. It was not conceived as a policy statement to be adhered to by the board and enforced among its members. On the contrary, it was developed as a sales pitch to be presented to the Pottstown Area Industrial Development group in support of its application for a $40,000 loan to insure the salary and benefits of the executive director for a period of six months. Nowhere in this document can one find a concrete and binding plan to assure the continued employment of this, now

---

[105] Memo from the Treasurer of the Pottstown Symphony Orchestra Association to its board officers with attached business plan and dated 26 April 2007.

prized, executive director following the expiration of this initial six month period. Phrases such as "has established an expanding list of potential major contributors" or "the nomination committee is aggressively working to fill the board with business leaders and professionals" or the statement that the rehiring of the previous executive director would "be instrumental in guiding the board out of debt", all preclude a tacit acceptance of the principles behind such statements.[106] As circumstance would have it, however, there was no serious intent behind any of this as we will see later in this narrative.

Eventually, the Pottstown Area Industrial Development group did grant a loan to the board for the requested $40,000. Upon being informed, the newly rehired executive director immediately began with the development of a multi-partite fund-raising plan which would involve all of the board members, the staff, its officers and others, engaging them in areas where they had competence and should have had myriad connections. In an earlier chapter, I have detailed the unwillingness of the board president to allow their previously hated executive director, whom they had now elevated to the role as their potential savior, to even present this plan. It was clear from the beginning that through the actions of the board officers in initially denying to him this opportunity to present a plan for debt removal, these officers had no intention other than to use his presence to rescue the substantial William Penn and several other grants from the rejection pile. Initially, this board required a rationale to continue as it had for years. The only problem was that it had run out of money and, very quickly, it was also running out of time.

With the help of several board members who pressured the board president and the officers to allow this exchange of ideas, the executive director was finally allowed to present this 20 point plan which was calculated to lead the orchestra out of debt. The principles of the plan were simple, i.e. each would concentrate on his or her own professional circles and use his or her supposed contacts in these circles to directly approach the CEO's, COO's and CFO's of major corporations. There was nothing complicated in the plan, only the overcoming of childish fears of rejection. Immediately following the presentation, word began to spread that the members of the board could not be expected to contact executives. They would do everything via the secretaries and managers with the corporations' marketing departments. Also, the board president and spouse of the headmaster of the Hill School patently refused to approach anyone in her circle even though she and her husband were in contact with major donors

---

[106] Ibid.

who gladly contributed to one of the wealthiest private boarding schools in the USA[107] and by doing so she would have helped insure the continued existence of the symphony, which was also one of the few cultural attractions that could also have been implemented as an element in the Hill School's recruitment efforts. At the very least were she to have stood by this position for reasons of personal ethics, she could have arranged for the symphony to have continued using the Hill School's auditorium for its performances without charge (in 2007, the Pottstown Symphony's budget projections announced an approximate total of $6,000 for hall rental and associated services), or arranged for a direct contribution by the school to the orchestra. She did neither of these. In a memo of 31 July 2007, the executive director, in frustration, wrote to the entire board: "To approach the gatekeepers is to invite rejection."[108] This warning went unheeded and the criticism grew for his impunity at proposing to this board that it should work towards debt reduction. For most of the members of this body, that was the sole responsibility of the executive director and not of the board.

During this period one of the board officers, the now assistant treasurer, approached the executive director with the demand that he should release the restricted funds given to the orchestra through the $10,000 Bard Foundation grant for the orchestra's educational program to the repayment of a loan he had made to the orchestra. The amount of that loan was $21,850 as had been reported on the orchestra's previous tax return. He argued that his wife was giving him problems regarding the sum and maintained that he had loaned the funds for the educational programs anyway. His proposed "deal" was his willingness to forgive the repayment of the remaining $11,850 of his loan were he to receive the entire Bard Foundation grant. In an aggressive exchange of emails, he demanded this money but the executive director refused to authorize turning over restricted funds desperately needed to continue the educational outreach program to satisfy a board member loan. Thereafter, superficially, nothing further happened. However, behind the scenes and unknown to most of those in the organization, it seems that the officers sought a way to claim their place in the last lifeboat should the weight of the symphony's ever increasing debt cause the ship to sink.

In late summer, 2007, a memo was circulated by a member of the board, an investment advisor in Pottstown, who announced that he had found an

---

[107] http://www.guidestar.org/FinDocuments/2011/231/352/2011-231352647-08420749-9.pdf.
[108] Memo of Executive Director to Pottstown Symphony Association board of directors dated 31 July 2007.

anonymous donor who was prepared to give to the Pottstown Symphony the sum of $50,000 for general debt reduction. There were no strings attached to this gift except that the donor must remain anonymous. It was clear that this individual making the donation had no connection to the orchestra and, most probably, was simply seeking the tax relief that would come from such a high quality gift to a nonprofit organization. Soon, however, the purpose of this donation changed. Suddenly, in the board meeting of 19 September 2007, the board president announced that the $50,000 donation was now targeted to "reduce long term debt beginning with all outstanding board member loans."[109] Further to this statement, it was added that "the money is not to be used for any outstanding account payables."[110] This provision alone begs the question: How could an anonymous donor with no previous or present association to the symphony have even known there were such board member obligations outstanding? Clearly there are only two possibilities which would lead to his making such a stipulation. Either this condition was added by the lending board members themselves, after the fact, and the donor had no knowledge of this limitation or the restriction of this amount primarily to the repayment of board member loans had been presented to the donor as of key importance to the organization at the expense of the outstanding payables and of the money due to the employees. Unless the anonymous donor had had a previous relationship to the symphony, something I do not believe was the case; he was clearly either duped into making this restriction or the restriction was imposed upon the donation by third parties and at a later time. This latter scenario gains weight through the failure of the board president to share the promised letter from the donor in which he supposedly clarified this condition. The board president had been requested to produce this donor initiated document on several occasions, by other board members and by the executive director. Each time she had an excuse for not doing so and promised that a copy would be forthcoming. The promised letter was never made available.

It was also at this meeting that a "Loan Agreement" document covering such board member credit was circulated. This document, prepared by the symphony's attorney, states that the "Director hereby agrees that the said Loan shall be forgiven, in the form of a gift, to the PSOA in the event of PSOA's dissolution."[111] From this language it is clear that the impending insolvency of the organization was prominent in the minds of those who

---

[109] Minutes of the Pottstown Symphony Orchestra Association from 19 September 2007.
[110] Ibid.
[111] Loan Agreement between Pottstown Symphony Orchestra Association and Members of its Board of Directors dated 15 October 2007.

stood to lose were the Pottstown Symphony Orchestra Association to enter default. The statement echoed in the 19 September 2007 minutes, that "the money be used to reduce long term debt beginning with all outstanding Board Member loans"[112] must be criticized in light of the agreement of 15 October and its handling of the ensuing indebtedness in the event of bankruptcy.

With this stroke, the outstanding board member loans amounting to $43,350 had been wiped clean but the continuing threats of litigation, the repeated warnings from the telephone company and countless vendors in the community and the indebtedness the organization had towards its own employees were not addressed. It is to be noted that, at this juncture, the board owed the music director over $2,000 in unreimbursed but approved travel costs since December of the previous year. Her complaint that she should finally and conclusively be repaid from this fund fell on deaf ears. In addition, it is to be added here that both the music director and her husband had repeatedly donated to the symphony in its times of need which makes this refusal to reimburse an employee for valid out-of-pocket expenses at a time when funds to do so were available, nothing less than a massed exercise in disrespect towards the music director and her contributions to the Pottstown Symphony's survival during lean periods. Of course, the about to expire funds from the PAID loan were also not considered in this equation although in the minutes of 16 September 2007, it clearly states that "the designated fund balance is $19,348.76."[113] These facts lead me to the decisive conclusion that the real purpose in repaying board member loans first was to rescue this select group from potential loss should the Pottstown Symphony Orchestra Association be compelled to declare bankruptcy. Neither the employees nor the symphony's outstanding creditors would receive any similar consideration. The $2,000 in expenses due the music director was finally paid to her thanks to an action initiated by the medical products executive who authorized this be taken from the season sponsorship fund provided by his company. It was at this meeting that the governance committee attached its impeachment proposals to the minutes of the discussions. There was no vote on this matter at this time. Without a vote, or even discussion among those on the full board, this same committee would use this unapproved document against a fellow board member who, by this time, was incensed at this blatant breach of trust surrounding the conditions imposed on the $50,000 anonymous donation, and do so fewer than nine days later. Also, the symphony's attorney who had said nothing about the

---

[112] Minutes of the Pottstown Symphony Orchestra Association Board of Directors' meeting from 19 September 2007.
[113] Ibid.

impeachment action this time endorsed the diversion of the $50,000 anonymous donation to satisfy the board member loans of his associates, having already drafted the loan agreement at the time the $50,000 had become available. It was reported by a board member who was also an officer and partner in the local insurance brokerage firm that this lawyer saw nothing wrong with this transaction. Many others on the board saw this differently and contested what clearly seemed to have been a redirection of the donation away from helping the symphony towards helping individuals should the symphony face bankruptcy.

Responding to the ever increasing pressure from unpaid creditors, the board decided, in October 2007, that it would increase the board member financial requirement to $10,000 each year. No sooner was this determined than a discussion ensued about what, exactly, a $10,000 board obligation would mean. Disregarding the onerous burden of debt they were carrying, this sum was quickly reduced from $10,000 to a maximum of $2,500 with $7,500 being offered as in-kind. How one would calculate the precise value of many in-kind contributions and offers of services which had, traditionally, been performed by board members anyway, was something that was never discussed. Later, this equation was further adjusted to credit certain board members, employees of companies which had made major donations, with the full value of their company's donation. In general, this would have presented no problems were it not for the further development of this tactic which diluted these donations further, spreading these amounts among any and all board members who had had anything at all to do with securing the donation. At the end of the day, nothing was changed.

Also in response to the increasing pressure the executive director and music director were putting on the board to commence work on the fund raising plans proposed and outlined by the executive director (at this stage there had now been two, detailed sets of plans proposed), a small group consisting of two investment brokers and the candidate recruited from "Business on Board" decided to host a fund-raising wine tasting party at a local art gallery in Phoenixville, Pennsylvania, an upscale community just east of Pottstown. They maintained that they had sent 1,000 invitations to their industry groups and that there had been no reply. However, it was in the nature of these invitations that the resulting failure of this action was pre-programmed. In September, the local Chamber of Commerce in Pottstown held one of its usual award breakfasts at which more than 500 invitees were in attendance. In preparation for this event, on the previous evening, the executive director went to the banquet room to assist the Chamber but also to place program booklets for the coming season of the Pottstown Symphony at each place setting. This was a customary and highly effective way of alerting many of the local businesses that there was still an opportunity to secure tickets and subscriptions and this tool had often resulted in donations. He received a telephone call that evening from the symphony's administrative assistant that one of the board members in this group was in the office and had left over 500 photocopies of the invitation to this wine tasting party and for him to please come and collect and to distribute at the place settings for the following morning's breakfast. It never occurred to any of the members of this group that, perhaps, this might have been their responsibility and, further, that the distribution of photocopied and wordy invitations showed no class whatsoever and invited instantaneous disdain at the initiative. It is probable that this rejection was exactly what they were seeking, a way to turn around this drive to force the board to fund raise and to show, conclusively, that these methods would not work. The desired result was achieved. Not a single business owner or any of those who had, supposedly, been contacted by this group bothered to react to the invitations which, in themselves, were off-putting and many at that breakfast gathering could have deemed to be insulting. Nonchalantly, the group simply announced to the board that they would gladly hold the event in any case but as a social event for the board alone. Even here, no one responded, not even the board members themselves.

It should be mentioned here that the two, extensive fundraising plans presented to the board by the executive director were not based on any new or experimental or radical ideas but on boilerplate principles that had functioned well for countless other organizations. A questionnaire was eventually distributed to the board by the executive director. It was his last hope that this group could be motivated into action. The board member who introduced the "show house" idea in 2006 returned vague answers indicating that he had "contacts". Thereafter, he disappeared from the board. The drama teacher and vice-president openly stated that she first had her school play and then was going on vacation. Considering that the president had also refused to work within either of these plans, or any other plan for that matter, this summarizes the quality of the Pottstown Symphony Orchestra Association's leadership at board level in time of crisis.

Meanwhile, the numbers of unpaid invoices was quickly taking a stranglehold on the organization. Upon his return to the Pottstown Symphony, in July 2007, the executive director had learned that the chamber music series he and the music director had created, an idea that raised money for the symphony, involved the unbridled cooperation of Emmanuel Lutheran Church, provided additional income for the musicians, was an outreach to senior citizens and to the handicapped in the region and which had not cost the symphony anything to achieve these goals, was suddenly in jeopardy of being cancelled by the church. The arrangement with Emmanuel and with the participating musicians was that each party would equally share in one-third of the proceeds for each concert. In general, this meant the payment of several hundred dollars to each party immediately following the concerts which, as a general rule, were also reasonably well attended. After his departure, in December 2006, these concerts had continued and the attendance levels had also been maintained. However, the symphony had, suddenly, ceased to return the agreed-to one-third share of the proceeds to the church. For many on the church council and the music committee of Emmanuel Lutheran, this was an affront. After all, they viewed the issue as one where, as had become customary, the proceeds were divided, in cash, following the concert and paid to the respective parties immediately. This saved anger and misunderstanding and preserved what the music director and executive director had created there, i.e. a trusting and healthy relationship with a historic church which had also been a bastion that upheld the Pottstown Symphony during its founding phase over 60 years before. It became the unpleasant duty of the executive director to smooth over this annoyance and to apologize to all concerned, even though he carried no responsibility for this opportunistic and unthinking behavior. Eventually the church was repaid, thanks to immense pressure put on the board by the executive director, and matters continued as before but the feeling within the church that the symphony was quite comfortable with cheating them was never fully eliminated. A year later, when the music director and executive director had left the scene, the then pastor of the church refused to work together with the symphony any longer. He had been burned once by their irresponsibility. A second occurrence was not something he chose to risk.

However, the issue of unpaid bills to major vendors did not stop with Emmanuel Lutheran Church. A former board member who had proposed bankruptcy months before and who, finally, left the organization in disgust when nothing happened to improve its finances, was also the owner of a major audio/video post-production studio in Philadelphia. He was a good friend of the music director and she had persuaded him to produce archive recordings of the Pottstown Symphony Orchestra concerts for potential broadcast on public radio but also for use in grants applications which he had also agreed to do at what one can easily call a "dumping price". For months, he had not been paid for recordings already made of previous concerts and was now threatening not to work for or with the Pottstown Symphony again. It was only a week or two before the opening concert of the season and, finally, the treasurer and partner in the insurance agency in town sent a plea to the board to personally write checks to cover the long in arrears $10,000 in open invoices, one of which was for the audio recordings.

Reacting in panic, several of the board members managed to scrape together sufficient funds to cover the bills for recording costs and a few other items but, as usual, the general lethargy among this group did nothing to change the situation.

In October, the $50,000 check from the anonymous donor was received and the board president requested the executive director to handle the matter. Upon reflection, he refused, protesting that he felt this assignment of funds at this time was a moral affront against those who had placed trust in the symphony. He repeated his position that the outstanding payables and the employees should be the first to be repaid. As of 19 October 2007, the symphony's outstanding payables amounted to $32,119 with a total lump sum due amounting to $124,336. There was no hint of any fundraising activity coming from this board anywhere on the horizon.

Reacting to strong protest by several on the board who were in opposition to this style of governance, the board president promised she would email the letter from the anonymous donor to everyone.[114] This was never done and repeated requests for photocopies of this letter, in which it was purported the donor clearly expressed his requirement that the board member loans be first satisfied, were never answered. The probability remains great that this letter never at all existed and that this was nothing but a scheme developed by the affected board members to recover their loans before the ship of the symphony sank under the ponderous weight of its debt and unfulfilled obligations.

Other matters such as warning notices regarding printing invoices from a company outside of Pottstown were accompanied by threats to send the amount due to collection. For months, the treasurer of the board and the board, itself, did nothing. Finally the executive director did succeed in making a repayment deal, in installments, which the vendor accepted. The payment schedule was adhered to for a while but, at the end, when there was no longer any one to monitor them, they, too, ceased to be made.

Most onerous of all, however, was the issue of over $10,000 in unpaid invoices due to the advertising company that had designed the look and maintained the web site for the Pottstown Symphony. An employee of this company, a young woman and graphic artist who was constantly at odds with the prevailing view of the board that fund raising was beneath them, also sat on the board of the symphony. She was a long-standing board member and had donated as much of her time as possible to creating advertising for the orchestra at no cost to the symphony. It would have been

---

[114] Minutes of the Pottstown Symphony Orchestra Association board meeting of 17 October 2007.

difficult, even at that closeness of time, to have put a dollar value on the savings she initiated for the organization but amounts in the tens-of-thousands-of-dollars would be a reasonable estimate of her value to the Pottstown Symphony. In addition, although her employer billed the orchestra for its professional services at times where the pro bono work of the artistic director was not possible, the advertising agency also offered the symphony a rebate of 10% following payment of each invoice. The outstanding bills, however, went back more than a year and it was beginning to look as if the symphony was prepared to throw this young woman and board member to the dogs by simply ignoring its obligation to this vendor and to her. The bookkeeper at the advertising agency alerted the executive director of the issues and he immediately realized the need to quickly satisfy this debt. Not to have done so could realistically have meant that the employee with association to the symphony board and with a family might have been held accountable by her employer. Since, as a board member, she was also in a decision making position within the symphony, the expectation that her employer would recognize and act upon her accountability in this matter was very high. Although the art director refuted this assertion, the executive director was quite concerned and pressured the board to quickly settle these invoices. The board did nothing. The problem was solved through use of a portion of the season sponsorship funds supplied by the medical systems company. This was done with the approval of the donor and with the knowledge of the board and its officers. Still, the bad taste remained. The readiness of this board to sacrifice one of its own on the altar of its own laziness and ineptitude permanently soured the relationships between the old guard and the increasingly vocal faction that was now calling for change.

There were also other instances such as the local school district demanding the rent for a holiday concert performed a year before and the dunning notices from the telephone company and from the health care provider and others. The list was endless and the standard excuse, "the check is in the mail" no longer satisfied anyone. There were vendors in Pottstown who simply accepted the problem as their loss and chalked it all up to Pottstown loyalty and there were the others, many from outside the region, who repeatedly threatened legal action. Nothing seemed to move this board to act, except where it would concern the repayment of their own board member loans. In view of these abuses it is not to be forgotten that by directing the $50,000 donation to the repayment of board member loans this board did so not only at the cost of the organization's creditors and the security of its employees but also at the cost of the US taxpayers who, by granting non-profit status through the Internal Revenue Service, renounced their claim to any tax income from this source and from investments made in the organization in the form of donations.

In November, one of the financial advisors on the board and owner of a company in Pottstown borough wrote to the music director: "What % (sic) are the annual subscription sales to costs for all concerts per season? What is the shortfall that needs to come from grants, sponsorships and or donations? This is not a complex business to run. We need to determine these two factors. In turn the grant writing needs to begin in HASTE to get something sustainable in the door long term to cover op (sic) expenses. Ideally the revenue to cover op (sic) expenses year should only come from TWO sources, Subscription and grants. All of the other sponsorship and donation money should be earmarked for building reserve balances for future programming expenses and…yes…An endowment."[115]

Despite countless hours of explanation as to how the revenue from tickets barely covers 10% of the costs, that higher ticket prices would cost the symphony a significant portion of its audience and the ensuing ticket revenue, and despite the explanation that the myriad grants applications this orchestra had completed were being rejected because the debt level was too high, this and the other board members chose to ignore these facts and fall back into a long disproven and simplistic formula. At least, in this case, there was recognition to some degree of the need for fundraising and ticket sales, even if that recognition was expressed in an oversimplified manner. It was the other investment broker, manager of a company in an affluent suburb who would never accept that ticket sales didn't cover all the revenue requirements of a symphony orchestra. Despite years of studying the orchestra's budget and commenting on the ensemble's expenses, he had failed until almost the very end to realize that professional musicians also must be paid.

Some of the musicians, however, had already begun to express worry about the Pottstown Symphony's ability to pay them. The executive director had calmed down several of these, concerned inquiries and, at one time had been offered a fundraising proposal by a player requiring the Pottstown Symphony to involve itself in a pyramid scheme selling "Indian Gobi Juice". It was clear from such proposals that, even then, the musicians had little idea of the seriousness of the situation within the symphony.

At this point, the financial end of the symphony was nearing rapidly. The representative of the medical products company and, himself, the internal auditor for that multinational concern, issued a memo to the entire board in early December 2007. Key in this memo was his expert analysis of the

---

[115] Memo of 12 November 2007 to Music Director.

situation which he summarized as follows: "MOST IMPORTANTLY – As I see it, we have no more than 60 days to come to grips with what will become an unmanageable deficit. Without an infusion, by the end of February, of at least $100K more than is currently anticipated, we may not be able to continue operating for the balance of the season and fiscal year. Even with such an infusion, we're likely facing a similar challenge as we look ahead to the 2008-09 fiscal year."[116]

The board president replied: "All of us need to press really hard"[117]. To that, the music director replied, somewhat cynically, "Are we making cookies – or are we playing rugby?"[118] At this stage, the lines of combat had been drawn and even the auditor who wrote this initial memo, as were many of those on the board and almost all of the employees, were convinced that this board and its officers were driving the symphony into ruin and that combative action had to be taken if this tragedy were to be avoided.

When, in February 2008, no action had been taken by the board and as the debt continued to rise, the executive director, in consultation with the author of the 07 December analysis memo, called together a meeting of the symphony's executive committee consisting of the president, vice-president, treasurer, assistant treasurer and two other board members, one of whom was the "Business on Board" appointee. He had prefaced this discussion by submitting a white paper to the officers in which he clearly laid out the alternatives the organization had were it to stay alive. These included the cancellation of concerts, the cancellation of the educational program, the non-payment to musicians and others (default), the engagement of an outside development company to secure funds (if possible), the immediate fulfillment of the board member financial obligations in cash plus a one-time mandatory contribution necessary to satisfy the debt or, as a last resort, default and bankruptcy. He also recommended that the presently constituted board dissolve itself and make room for a competent body consisting of philanthropically minded and generous, arts interested business persons.[119] There was little reaction except from the former treasurer and now, assistant treasurer expressing his thought that someone should contact Oprah Winfrey and ask her for help. He was serious in this suggestion. Neither the music director nor the executive director, both of whom were present, took this suggestion as any more than an expression of hopelessness.

---

[116] Memo from internal auditor to PSOA board dated 07 December 2007.
[117] Memo from Board President of the PSOA to the Board of Directors dated 07 December 2007.
[118] Ibid. Reply of 07 December 2007.
[119] Executive Director memo to board officers from 26 February 2008.

A month later, in March 2008, the Nonprofit Finance Fund of Philadelphia conducted an audit of the Pottstown Symphony's finances. The executive director had initiated this as a last-ditch effort to convince the board and its officers that they had to finally react to the crisis. Four board members, the music director, a fundraising consultant and the administrative assistant for the orchestra were present. The executive director was ill at the time and grateful that he would have no input into what he anticipated would be the dramatic conclusions taken by the NFF. From this report, it was made clear that the origins of the problem began almost 10 years before, with the drive to become a regional instead of a local orchestra. In the years between 2001 and 2007, with one exception, the ensemble posted operating deficits. The report also stated that during this period, the symphony did not generate sufficient revenue to support its desired expansion, that the limited staff infrastructure created an untenable burden and that the orchestra has operated throughout the period without a cushion, developing an increasingly negative net worth with existing cash balances designated only for specific purposes. In addition, the unrestricted operating results after depreciation show a recurrence of negative numbers with the sole exception of the year 2003 where the symphony operated at a 21% profit. This finding was accompanied by the comment that "while the organization generated an unrestricted surplus in 2003, the total change in net assets was -$62,000 as a result of changes in temporary restricted activities. As a result, total assets declined during 2003."[120] Between 2001 and 2005, the investment picture for the Pottstown Symphony had been reduced to zero. In 2004, cash was at its all-time low with nothing on the horizon to compensate for the losses. With the engagement of a full-time music director and executive director, despite the now abandoned and special "Mr. X" fund, the liabilities increased to over $140,000 by the end of 2007 and support for the organization was rapidly dwindling while professional fees were climbing. It was clear that this report was presenting the picture of an organization beyond rescue.

Evidently, in a band aid approach to the solution of the debt issue, both the former treasurer, himself vice-president of a local bank and the newly elected board vice-president each committed themselves to further board member loans totaling, respectively, $7,500 and $5,000. In addition, the insurance company executive loaned the organization another $7,500 and an examination of the IRS form I-990 from the fiscal year ending 30 June 2008, shows that the bank manager who was to be repaid the loan of $1,500 he had advanced to the symphony, may have forfeited this repayment as a result of

---

[120] Nonprofit Finance Fund report from March 2008, page 13.

the negative feedback that came from the restrictive and suspicious nature of the anonymous $50,000 donation.

The issue of funding the symphony reached its zenith in April, 2008, when seeing insufficient funding available to pay the musicians hired for a series of educational concerts, both executive director and music director threatened to cancel these performances rather than have their reputations damaged by a default on these amounts unless the symphony officers could guarantee that the funds for these concerts were now available. In a telephone call with the then assistant treasurer, the executive director and the music director were assured by the assistant treasurer that the symphony had amassed the sum of $27,900 in, as he put it, "hard dollars" which would easily cover the anticipated payroll which would have been $41,400 and that the remaining $13,500 would come from the fees paid by the participating school districts. Remember, the educational outreach concerts were performed, annually and in April for audiences amounting to about 10,000 children. Of the cited $27,900 in "hard dollars" which, presumably, was in the hands of the Pottstown Symphony Orchestra Association, it is important to realize that $10,000 came from the notorious Bard Foundation grant which this board member had tried to commandeer for himself in repayment of his board member loan. There was no truth to this statement made by the assistant treasurer, as both the music director and executive director would soon discover. In addition, seeing the opportunity to, finally, take revenge on both the music director and executive director, certain and former members of the board, including the former president, sabotaged agreed upon children's concerts in the educational outreach series which further reduced the income from these concerts and guaranteed a deficit from them.

The organization had ruptured and, at the end of April, the music director, executive director, several board members including the one representing the symphony's season sponsor, the art director, the personnel contractor and others resigned their positions. There was a brief encore played out in the halls of the Pennsylvania Unemployment Compensation Review Board in which the verdict of the referee confirmed the verdicts of so many who had gone before: "The board of directors hired the claimant to expand the orchestra in order to create a regional presence. The claimant sought to meet the conditions agreed to at the beginning of employment, over the years, however, the claimant learned that the board was not prepared to do as agreed. The claimant found that the board made fiscally irresponsible decisions, continued to mount an increasing deficit and did not implement plans to overcome the deficit…The claimant implored the board to take action."[121]

In 2009, the regular contributions made by the County of Montgomery General Appropriations fund were cancelled. This cost the Pottstown Symphony a further $10,000 in lost revenue.

Sometime in 2008, the board of directors made an attempt at securing financial liability insurance for its members. The application was denied even though one of the board members was also a partner in a local insurance brokerage firm. Considering the massive amount of debt the symphony carried, one can only imagine the reasons for this refusal. One simply doesn't insure a burning barn!

Prior to January 2010, the symphony had performed its usual holiday concerts which, traditionally under the former music director, had been sold out. A musician who worked those concerts reported: "Apparently no payment to musicians has been made as yet for Messiah (early December) as well as no payment for the holiday concert (mid-December). This past weekend's efforts apparently drew a crowd Saturday night at the Hill of c. 125-150 [capacity close to 700], and the repeat performance at Ursinus College on Sunday drew all of 25 in the audience. Apparently [the board president – the PSO had elected yet another one, the drama teacher, as successor to the headmaster's wife] did a pre-concert spiel Saturday evening, asking for money and confessing to the crowd that the concert had no corporate sponsor."[122]

As to the legacy left behind by the former president and spouse of the headmaster of the Hill School, the "Hill School Community Impact Statement 2010-2011" which covered the activities and cooperative efforts undertaken by the school in their 2009-10 fiscal year, betrays no serious efforts by the school to assist the Pottstown Symphony during these, critical, final days except for the following statement: "The Center For The Arts hosts and provides free or below-cost rental of facilities to the following: Pottstown Symphony Orchestra, Tri-County Chamber of Commerce, Schuylkill Valley Regional Dance Company, area artists' exhibits, Coventry Players, and Pottstown Community Band, YWCA."[123] As noted earlier, despite the presence of the Pottstown Symphony's board president on the faculty of the school, until the year 2008 the use of this facility by the

---

[121] Unemployment Compensation Board of Review, Referee's Decision/Order from 13 August 2008.
[122] Memo from 11 January 2010 sent from former Music Director to former Executive Director.
[123] "The Hill School Community Impact Statement 2010-2011", page 5.

symphony had not been contributed to the organization, even in times of the symphony's most dire need. At best, it seems that at this stage following the year 2008, the Pottstown Symphony was allowed to use the facility at a discounted rate. However, the fact that by the advent of the year 2010, the Pottstown Symphony had effectively cancelled all activities which would have required use of a concert hall, this discounted rate would have been of no use in improving the orchestra's fiscal condition.

In June, 2010, the Pottstown Symphony hired a new music director on a five year contract. The position had been vacant since May 2008. Where the symphony expected to find the money to pay for his services is a question that went unanswered.

In a memo from 29 May 2012, Rebecca Vierhaus, Director of Member Services with the League of American Orchestras, responded to an inquiry by this author as follows: "The Pottstown Symphony Orchestra's membership did lapse last year [expired 30 September 2010], so they aren't currently members of the league."[124]

The "PottstownSymphonyOrchestra.org" domain name never did belong to the symphony but to the former orchestra manager who had loaned the ensemble $19,000 as described at the beginning of this chapter. For more than a year this domain name had been available for sale with an asking price of $2,500.[125]

---

[124] Email from Rebecca Vierhaus of the League of American Orchestras to Kevin Wood dated 29 May 2012.
[125] https://www.buydomains.com/EnterContactInfo.do?domain=pottstownsymphony.org&utm_source=TDFS&utm_medium=sn_affiliate_click&utm_campaign=TDFS_Affiliate_Endurance&traffic_id=Endurance&traffic_type=TDFS&referrer_id=4785. Sometime at the beginning of 2014, the Pottstown Symphony Orchestra's domain name was, indeed, sold to an organization in Japan. The headline on that web site, to be found under www.pottstownsymphony.org, reads "I go through life in obscurity".

6. MARKETING AND THE PUBLIC

It would be fair to say that the marketing of the Pottstown Symphony to its existing constituencies and the approach to potential, future constituencies was already in disarray prior to the year 2005. It was clear that the organization had no understanding of why an arts organization engages in marketing nor did it understand what the expected results would or should have been from that effort. A simple and factual definition of this function of doing business would have gone a long way towards preventing the misunderstandings and wrong moves and flawed decisions that came from both the board and, sometimes, also from the symphony's staff.

A well-accepted and straightforward definition of why an arts organization needs to market was given by the analyst, Philip Kotler. According to Mr. Kotler, marketing within the arts is "the analysis, planning, implementation, and control of carefully formulated programs designed to bring about voluntary exchanges of values with target markets for the purpose of achieving organizational objectives."[126]

With the acceptance of Mr. Kotler's clarification, it becomes also clear that the marketing function of an arts organization is inseparably tied to the organization's strategic plan. In Pottstown, however, the marketing was viewed by the board as a separate entity to be used to draw audiences into concerts. Although the management team consisting of the music director and the executive director knew that this focus was wrong, they also became caught-up in this "sales" mentality partially because they viewed an increase in patron numbers as reflecting an increased interest in the symphony and as a fundraising mechanism. Not that this concept was wrong in itself. The problem with this thinking was the unwillingness to take into account the disrepute into which the board, and by extension the association, had fallen. The role of an effective and targeted marketing concept would, certainly, have fulfilled that objective and resulted in this awakening of interest in the orchestra had these other factors not muddied the waters of public sentiment and had the community itself, as represented by its politicians, stood behind the effort. However, it would have done much more. A properly organized marketing objective could also have carried much value towards the elimination of the ensemble's weighty burden of debt and would have generated interest in the orchestra from outside the region.

---

[126] Philip Kotler: *Strategic Marketing for Nonprofit Organizations* (New York: Prentice Hall, 1995).

It is precisely this issue that Lambert Zuidervaart addresses in his study of politics, economics and democratic culture. Zuidervaart discusses at length what he refers to as "Merit Good Arguments" where "the need to regard artistic practices as important in their own right points us toward merit good arguments for government arts funding. Yet, unlike efficiency and equity arguments, merit good arguments have an uncertain status in mainstream economics because economists disagree about the content and legitimacy of the concept of merit goods."[127] In short, the perception of why one donates to the arts and the fundamental need to finance artistic initiatives relies upon the same logical processes which determine how and why the arts should be marketed. This begs the question as to whether the arts and an artistic institution are a service or a product. Clearly, as a product the consumption of music assumes a greater value. However, the definition of art as a service gives to it a transcendental status which, alas, we have seen as the rationale in our digital age for the unscrupulous theft of downloaded intellectual property. It was exactly this flawed rationale that lay at the core of the Pottstown Symphony's thinking and which reached its apex in the "free" holiday concerts to be discussed later in this narrative.

In addition to this problem, which we will address in this chapter in greater detail, the do-it-yourself board of the Pottstown Symphony had never understood the importance of customer service as a means with which to win confidence in the organization. After all, in the case of any cultural organization, the role of any marketing or customer service initiative is to do exactly that, to win the trust and confidence of the public. I have already detailed the story of the board member assigned to ticket sales who, prior to 2006, would simply ask anyone ordering tickets to please leave their name, address, order specifics and credit card information on an answering machine and the order would, at some point, be fulfilled. Whether this occurred in an accurate or inaccurate fashion and how many customer service complaints there may have been before 2006, is a statistic I do not have. What, however, can be demonstrated is that the initiation of a computerized system of self-ordering after 2006, along with a presence in the symphony office of persons who took an interest in customer satisfaction, resulted in a first year increase in ticket sales of about 9% and that the further refinement of that system in the following year, with the introduction of a self-generating ticketing system, increased this further to where, at the end of 2007, the Pottstown Symphony could claim a 13% increase in seasonal ticket sales. It must be noted here that there was not that

---

[127] Lambert Zuidervaart: *Art in Public* (New York: Cambridge University Press, 2011).

much more room for growth in these numbers and it would have taken a quantum leap in new subscription and single ticket orders to have had further and significant impact on the bottom line. Properly organized and with a reasonably secure financial foundation, this could have been accomplished. In 2007, the Pottstown Symphony was playing its classical concerts to houses at 95% capacity. The holiday concerts which, under the old regulations in force prior to 2007, had been offered without admission charge, suffered under the widespread public impression that anything that can be gotten for free is also worthless. People would acquire the complimentary tickets and then not attend which resulted in dissatisfaction among those who were unable to secure passes to these concerts. The change in procedure initiated at the insistence of the music director and the executive director and which, after 2007, put a minimal price tag on each ticket, not only resulted in increased income for the symphony but also in people viewing these concerts as something of value. The simple idea that when one pays for something, it acquires tangibility actually increased the audience numbers and the revenue for the holiday season events.

In short, the classical and holiday concerts could only have benefitted from a quantum leap in ticket orders which would have forced a repeat of, or in the case of the holiday programs further repeats of each concert performance. This would have required an increase of something close to 400 to 500 tickets sold for each classical concert, if not more, since the concert hall at the Hill School where the symphony performed was a smaller theatre with a capacity of about 700 seats. In this region and at this time, a change of venue to a larger concert hall would not have been an option. There was simply enough, no theater with significantly increased capacity available to the orchestra. The closest large concert halls would have been in Reading or in Philadelphia and both were home to other, significant symphony orchestras and well outside of the greater Pottstown region. It would have alienated the Pottstown public and been politically incorrect to even consider using these venues, especially the one in Reading, which would have also escalated the growing rivalry that had developed between Pottstown and that orchestra.

In the years subsequent to 2004 or 2005, the pops concerts began to suffer from poor attendance figures. Although the population was, essentially, blue-collar, it was exactly this public that couldn't afford the ticket prices for a pops performance with symphony orchestra. In 2008, tickets for these concerts were being sold at the prices of $40 for adults and $35 for senior citizens. Compared to the ticket prices for the entirely classical "Masterworks" series which offered seats at $30 for adults, $25 for seniors and $10 for students, there seemed to be a disconnect between the need to pay the operating costs for a pops concert (often these were higher because the soloists were also often more expensive) and the realization that the middle class, blue-collar public simply didn't have the available cash with which to entertain such a luxury. In 2008, the international recession had begun and the troubling poverty statistics in the USA were starting to get worse. In an article published in 2012, the German magazine, Stern, reported on the alarming increase of poor and low-income families in the US.[128] In the year 2000, 11.3% of the population lived in poverty. By 2008, that number had increased to 15.1% and was on the rise. Also, the number of persons holding low-paying jobs amounted to an alarming 41% of the population while the average wage, adjusted for inflation, had decreased by 27% for males between the ages of 30 and 50. In a region such as Pottstown, plagued by poverty and criminality, the attendance at a symphonic pops concert would have fallen to the very bottom of anyone's list of unnecessary luxuries. The solution to this dilemma would have been simple but the board refused to accept the rationale of fundraising as a means with which to spread the message of the symphony to a wider audience. It would have been possible to have lowered these prices for the pops events by aggressive and organized fundraising campaigns launched in the interests of the symphony's general fiscal health and well-being. As with all arts organizations, the meeting of budget expectations should have been viewed as a satisfaction of the overall expectation for the season and not, as was so often done in Pottstown, as the need to cover the costs for single events. There was, simply enough, never a genuine business plan in place for the symphony despite the presence of two bankers and two financial advisors on the board. Any attempt by the executive director to compile such a plan would have been rejected out of hand. As was customary with almost all proposals made by the "paid staff", they were disregarded as coming from an "inferior" source. Of course, the dramatic debt picture in 2008 would have made this change of thinking somewhat difficult since the need to satisfy older payables, the increased dunning by long-term creditors and the requirement to simultaneously continue the current season was simply a burden the board was not in the position to shoulder.

However, the most serious problem confronting the Pottstown Symphony was one of credibility which the adoption of a certain codex of behavior could have nicely addressed as well as of a redefined sense of where and to whom the symphony "belonged". This issue was one that was never answered in a satisfactory fashion. There were those on the board who believed the symphony belonged to them and others, loyalists to Pottstown,

---

[128] Article: "Zur Lage der Nationen" (The State of the Union). (STERN: No. 11 08 March 2012, pages 48-49.

who believed that the orchestra belonged to the community but in a manner that gave precedence to a proprietary ownership instead of to a belonging in a broader, regional sense. For a short time, there was a weight of opinion that stood behind changing the name of the orchestra from "Pottstown Symphony" to some other, more regionally effective and less burdensome appellation. There were those on the symphony board, as well as the music director and executive director, who immediately understood the negative consequences of trying to fulfill the mandate of the board to make of this orchestra a regional one while retaining a name that confirmed the ensemble's allegiance to a dying community which had long lost the glitter of 50 years before. Pottstown was well on its way to becoming, at least economically and cosmetically, a ghost town. Already, in 2005, the numbers of vacant storefronts as one drove along High Street, the main thoroughfare through the town, was beginning to reach alarming proportions. On the side streets ruled a spreading culture of sex and drugs and organizations were starting to warn of the rapid growth in slums and of the prevalence of slumlords. This was no atmosphere in which to try and develop a symphony orchestra into a regional presence.

Had the symphony acted in a similar fashion as did the staff with respect to its payment morality and its outreach to the customers at the board level, the probability exists that it would also have found a more ready and accepting public at its disposal, prepared to donate to an institution that behaved morally and with transparency.

The general marketing of the organization was conducted with insufficient funds and little board co-operation. In fact, in the 2004-2005 concert season budget, there is not even a line item covering marketing and public relations costs. At that time, the design and much of the copywriting as well as the conceptualization of any strategies to sell the symphony were developed by the art director at the regional advertising agency who was also a member of the board and by the music director. This was part of the Pottstown Symphony's home-grown style. Even though it had hired a music director two years previously who came to the symphony with international credentials, the need to market this orchestra for and with its desired image doesn't seem to have been a priority. However, the art director was unusually creative and open to ideas and produced advertising and brochures for the symphony which were extraordinary in their effectiveness, directness and general impact. Aside from the musical excellence the Pottstown Symphony enjoyed under its new conductor, the second best reason for the high attendance figures during that time was the quality of the marketing done by the board-member, art director with the input of the music director.

By 2005 the picture within the symphony had begun to change. After three years in the job, the music director had begun to see the fraying edges in the board profile and to realize the hopeless situation caused by a continued loyalty to Pottstown as a community. Perhaps some of this realization came from the new executive director who began his work in Pottstown in October of that year. It had taken little time for the newly hired executive director to realize that this orchestra was operating under preconceptions which had lost their validity 20 years before. The music director wrote to the then treasurer of the organization, a banker who was also chairman of the Pottstown Symphony's strategic planning committee: "I am very concerned that the board of directors of the Pottstown Symphony lacks the appropriate skills, knowledge and understanding to run a professional orchestra. A limited sense of direction fueled by inadequate leadership has combined to create a general atmosphere of frustration and inertia…The immediate community does not actively support an orchestra in all the ways necessary to properly sustain and validate PSO's continued presence in Pottstown. Forty-two years of being the Pottstown Symphony Orchestra – and all the while fighting financial ruin – indicate not only the need to seriously consider changing locus, but to adopt a name that reflects the broader region the PSO in fact serves…Audience development will reap the rewards of an appropriate name change, continued broadening of concert location in the tri-county area and proper board requirements…All future seasons must be designed by the music director in conjunction with the executive director and presented for board approval by January/February, followed by [the] printing of [a] seasonal brochure in March with distribution to the mailing list and general public by March/April."[129]

Of course, in such a structure as the music director describes, fear of criticism remained paramount in the minds of the board members. In the case of this one board member who was then chairman of the strategic planning committee and entrusted with exactly this implementation of change, this fear of consequences should he initiate or suggest change, was to be seen in every action he took. On the same day, he had written to the members of his committee: "Board members have been encouraged to send comments and concerns to me prior to the meeting. I will compile and share any thoughts received anonymously."[130] I fail to see any advantage the Pottstown Symphony Orchestra Association would have gained from this anonymity apart from affording to single board members the opportunity to

---

[129] Memo from the Music Director of the Pottstown Symphony to the organization's Treasurer dated 17 November 2005.
[130] Memo from the Treasurer and Chairman of the Strategic Planning Committee of the Pottstown Symphony to the committee members dated 17 November 2005.

hide behind such a veil, using that veil to initiate further, this time anonymous attacks against the staff. At very least it can be said that such behavior does not encourage dialogue but, perhaps, that was exactly the purpose of this anonymity.

It is interesting to note that the name change initiative within the Pottstown Symphony grew in strength and influence as the symphony's debt began to mount. In 2005, 2006 and 2007, as well as in the preceding years, the political establishment in Pottstown, beginning with the mayor and going through the entire of Borough Council, systematically declined to offer the symphony any sort of financial or other support. It is to be recalled here, that this same political establishment had generously contributed to the founding of the orchestra under Kenneth Morse. Had the true origins of the Pottstown Symphony been recognized by the board and made known to politicians and public alike, this information could have given the Pottstown Symphony Orchestra the leverage it needed to change these attitudes within Borough Council.

Even though the case had been often made that investments in cultural organizations bring to communities an estimated $3 in tax revenues for each dollar spent on tickets, this argument fell, in Pottstown, on deaf ears. Also ignored was the statement of the National Endowment for the Arts that "…for every dollar the U.S. Treasury foregoes per tax deduction, donors are motivated to give private nonprofits an additional donation in the range of 90 cents to $1.40, according to recent estimates."[131] The organization, Americans for the Arts, published a survey of the economic impact of an artistic organization on a community in 2003. Entitled *Arts and Economic Prosperity*, this groundbreaking study did reveal several points which would have conclusively supported the community becoming a partner in the preservation of the symphony. In this report it was written: "When governments increase their support for the arts, they are generating tax revenues, jobs, and the creative energies that underlie much of what makes America so extraordinary." and, later in the report: "The nonprofit arts, unlike most industries, leverage significant event-related spending by their audiences, with non-local audiences spending 75 percent more than their local counterparts. The arts attract visitors downtown and extend the business day: restaurants add dinner service, garages stay open until midnight, and stores draw more customers."[132] Furthermore, later in this

---

[131] National Endowment for the Arts: "How The United States Funds the Arts" Washington, DC. 2007, page18.
[132] Americans for the Arts: "Arts and Economic Prosperity". *Washington, DC. 2003.* Page 6

same report, the advantages of both private sector and public sector support for an organization like the Pottstown Symphony are made even clearer. The report states how "the arts have proven to be a magnet for travelers and their money. Local businesses are able to grow because travelers extend the length of their trips to attend cultural events. Research by the Travel Industry Association of America and Partners in Tourism indicate that 65 percent of all adult travelers included a cultural event while on a trip of 50 miles or more away from home in 2000, 32 percent of which extended the duration of their trip because of that event. Of the group that extended their trip because of arts and culture, 57 percent extended their trip one or more nights. Travelers who include cultural events on their trips differ from other U.S. travelers in a number of ways. Compared to all U.S. travelers in 2001, cultural travelers: spend more ($631 vs. $457), are older (48 vs. 46), are more likely to be retired (20% vs. 16%), are more likely to have a graduate degree (23% vs. 20%), to use hotel, motel, or B & B (62% vs. 56%), are more likely to spend $1,000 or more (18% vs. 12%), will generally travel longer (5.2 nights vs. 4.1 nights), often travel by air (22% vs. 18%), and are much more likely to shop (44% vs. 33%) ". [133] All these points not only underscore the oft maintained $3 to $1 ratio described earlier in this narrative but also suggest that, in some communities, the benefits to the local governments may be even greater. In fact, the evaluation of the National Endowment for the Arts was even more optimistic. In a 2007 publication, the NEA states: "Every dollar that the NEA gave in grants typically generated seven to eight times more money in terms of matching grants, further donations, and earned revenue...The reason for this multiplying effect is obvious: NEA funding has the power to legitimize a new organization."[134] It was in 2007 that the Pottstown Symphony Orchestra received, exactly, this "legitimization" being awarded a $10,000 grant from the NEA. This was the first and only time the organization would be so recognized. Also, the results documented in the Charities Aid Foundation "Briefing Paper" of November, 2006, a set of findings that had been made known to both the Pottstown Symphony Board and to the Chamber of Commerce, were all ignored. In this briefing paper several facts which affect giving patterns in poorer communities and in the USA as a whole were laid out as part of the general action plan for more effective fundraising. The two most important findings for the Pottstown Symphony were the documented percent of giving based on the national and regional Gross Domestic Product and the tendency of the poorer strata of society, when motivated, to donate higher proportions of their income than

---

[133] Ibid. page 13.
[134] National Endowment for the Arts: "How the United States Funds The Arts". Washington, DC 2007. Page vii.

do the rich. In these cases, the average level of giving in the USA, pro capita, amounted to 1.6% of the nation's GDP. [135] The head of Pottstown's Tri-County Chamber of Commerce, a person for whom such statistics should have belonged to her basic knowledge of the business environment, was also negative in her feelings about the symphony. Never once did she seem to have explored the obvious benefits of encouraging Pottstown based businesses to support the orchestra. She seemed to consciously ignore the facts that "the increased visibility of a company's name and logo leads to increased brand recognition throughout the community. An easily recognized brand makes closing sales all the more effortless. Increased sales equal increased revenue" and "when a business donates to worthy local causes, such as those that fight poverty or disease, as well as cultural institutions, such as the ballet, opera or art museum, its image is often enhanced in the public's perception. No longer considered as simply a profit seeking corporation, a business' investment in the community signals a commitment and concern for its neighbors. Many consumers make purchasing decisions based upon this quality. Residents of a community will often show favor to local businesses. In many cases, they will go out of their way to support companies that support that community".[136] It is not known if the Chamber's executive director, once in her tenure, had bothered to attend a symphony concert or taken the time to study the impact of the arts on a community. This is also somewhat reflected in the PAID loan which went to the symphony to re-engage the executive director. The funding could have easily been offered as part of a community revitalization grant. Instead, it came in the form of an interest bearing loan. The executive director of the Chamber of Commerce echoed the opinion of the local newspaper, the Pottstown Mercury, which went out of its way not to report on Pottstown Symphony events. The then publisher of the newspaper and his editor were anything but interested in what they seemed to regard as an elitist activity. With the departure of the publisher in 2007, his replacement expressed somewhat more interest in the symphony but the damage to the organization in Pottstown through the disregard of the community's politicians, the local newspaper with its failure to report, critically, on the ensemble or to show much interest in it at all and representatives of the business community had been done. An attempt by the executive director, in 2008, to interest the Pottstown Mercury in engaging a free-lance concert

---

[135] Charitable Aid Foundation:" International Comparisons of Charitable Giving", November 2006.
[136] http://smallbusiness.chron.com/advantages-corporations-sponsoring-charitable-organizations-503.html.

reviewer failed for lack of funds and for want of an available and qualified person who was not connected with the orchestra.

Following the departure of the executive team and much of the board from the organization, in 2008, and the Pottstown's Symphony's return to its Pottstown identity with its new emphasis on the orchestra being a part of a "Positively Pottstown" movement, the remaining board members approached the Borough of Pottstown for financial assistance. Although the old guard on the board, knowing that the town in which they lived and which was home to the symphony had never shown any interest at all in the organization (most of them would have been unaware of Mr. Morse's part of this history), they wagered one last time on the sympathy of the Borough Council and presented a plan to the town in which it emphasized that the symphony had now focused its efforts on the immediate Pottstown area. The board president "made a presentation to council on July 9 in which she asked for both an endorsement of the symphony's new efforts and a contribution. And despite an agenda listing that indicated council would be voting Monday on both an endorsement and a contribution, the symphony only got half of what it was asking for…Council unanimously approved the resolution authorizing a letter of endorsement 'in support of its programming and fundraising.'…by the July 14 meeting, it became evident that the only support the symphony will receive from Borough Council is a letter."[137]

From this distance, this author is of the opinion that, even for the Borough Council, "Positively Pottstown" communicated a wrong and completely meaningless message. It is doubtful, knowing the Pottstown Symphony Orchestra Association's history with the Pottstown Borough Council, that the orchestra would have received any help from them; however, perhaps a slogan such as "Positive about Pottstown" might have stood a better chance with this group and left a better impression on the city fathers. The Borough of Pottstown was also a factor in the symphony's financial misery. It has been shown that, except for the one moment of enlightenment in the 1940's when the Recreation Commission helped to underwrite the founding of the symphony, the town fathers consistently refused any financial support for the ensemble, even in its last days. However, the Pottstown Borough Council had struck an even greater blow to the community and to the symphony by rejecting the introduction of commuter light-rail into the town even though the rights-of-way already existed and freight trains barreled through Pottstown on an almost hourly basis. Both the Pottstown Mercury in the

---

[137] Evan Brandt: "Orchestra gets council support for renewed fundraising drive". Pottstown Mercury from 16 July 2008, pages 1 and 3.

year 2010 and the PA Independent in 2011 recognized this flawed reasoning. The Pottstown Mercury wrote: "It was disappointing, to say the least, that Pottstown Borough Council voted to reject a plan that talks about providing many of the very things needed to revitalize this town. For more than 10 years, experts from Washington to Harrisburg to Philadelphia have been exposing the scourge of sprawl, how it hollows out cities of business, employers and the middle class residents who depend on them, how it overtaxes school systems and over-extends crumbling infrastructure. Organizations like First Suburbs are trying to buck this trend. But despite efforts to bring this effort to Pottstown, both physically and philosophically, the leadership here continues to have difficulty seeing beyond its own borders. What was before council last week was the opportunity to vote for a plan that calls for driving development and transportation dollars into established towns in order to attract private investment that will hopefully help make those places vibrant again. The Route 422 Master Plan, for which the Montgomery County Planning Commission was seeking endorsement, focuses on all the initiatives council has said are needed – economic development in towns, better infrastructure, rail service...As the Urban Land Institute effort so immediately recognized after only two days in town, the primary reason for Pottstown's failure to make progress on many of the thorny issues it faces is its inability to get out of its own way."[138]

A further rationale behind this decision, one to be heard on the streets of Pottstown, was the mistaken belief that such easy access to the community would introduce elements of prostitution and drug trafficking into the town. No one wanted to notice that these elements were already present. Such a rail link would have made of Pottstown a genuine commuter town, bringing money in the form of increased business, and would have introduced to the Pottstown Symphony the potential of a new, broad, better-educated and more affluent audience. The 2011 evaluation of the local Republican State Representative, Tom Quigley, failed to recognize the growth factor in ridership associated with such a plan. He commented to the PA Independent: "When you actually whittle it down, it looks like a much lower number of people will actually use the train"[139] The State Representative also commented how he had "received 20 emails and at least as many phone calls in opposition to the plan".[140]

---

[138] Editorial: "Council Objection to 422 Plan Proves Lack of Foresight". The Pottstown Mercury, 15 August 2010.
[139] PA Independent, 15 September 2011.
[140] Ibid.

With the decision of the Borough Council to continue its long-standing position and ignore the symphony, the failed marketing efforts of the remaining board members, those who had resisted change which might have saved the organization from ruin, had reached their zenith. However, there was still more to come.

In the following season the symphony board decided to open the lobby of the Hill School theatre during a concert performance to exhibits and presentations by other, local non-profits. In doing this, under the moniker "Positively Pottstown" they were trying to make points within this small community. In fact, what they were accomplishing was simply to further weaken a precarious financial position by opening their few remaining fundraising sources and their public to an equally desperate, and to some extent mercenary, competition. In and of itself, the "Positively Pottstown" argument, that the orchestra consisted only of musicians from the greater Pottstown area, flew in the face of the historical reality which had been recognized even as early as the 1940s, i.e., that Pottstown simply could not offer enough qualified professional musicians to sustain a symphony orchestra beyond the status of a community ensemble. Even the much touted William Lamb had brought players to Pottstown from Philadelphia, Baltimore and New Jersey.

Prior to all this, however, and before the final break which would see the departure of the music director, the executive director and half of the board, the name change initiative had begun to gain traction. A committee was formed with the advice of a marketing expert, volunteered from a large chemical company with headquarters in the region, who tried to guide the management staff and the board through the difficult task of finding and agreeing upon a suitable new name for the orchestra. Among themselves, the members of this committee had also given credibility to the need to keep its historical continuity and had asked the son of the former Music Director, Porter Eidam, if he would also assist with the finding of a new name. It was Porter Eidam senior who had begun to realize the problems in the name Pottstown Symphony. However, for him it was much too soon to also tackle such a hopeless task as would have been such a name change. This was especially true almost 10 years before. An interesting aside, however, is the comment made by the son of the now deceased former music director to the executive director in an email dated 08 January 2008. He wrote: "If you are interested in some "legacied (sic) input", I can quote my old man directly...'If Joe Smith wants to give us 5 million dollars a year with the stipulation that we call it the Joe Smith Orchestra, then goddammit I'm the conductor of the Joe Smith Orchestra'"[141]

Evidently, however, the momentum behind this action began to wane following an initial test phase where a series of potential new names was given to members of a county choral society. The sampling for this test phase was wrong and bore no similarity to the eventual target group which would (or would not) have accepted the new name for the symphony. The members of this choral society were all students but they sought the input of their parents as well, many of whom were adverse to any change of any kind with respect to the symphony and its identity. Of course, it must be remarked here that almost none of those who reacted negatively to the name change possibilities had donated or even subscribed to the orchestra and, as such, had no proprietary attachment to the orchestra except to slavishly hold on to the "Pottstown" identity.

Only 17 of 100 of these surveys were returned and, based on that meager sampling, the then assistant treasurer and board member and banker complained to the music director and executive director that "the students thought the name choices given were so poor that they didn't warrant a response... [He] said that these parents gave him the list of names, and he had a negative reaction to the list also."[142]

That was the last, serious action taken towards finding a marketable new name for the Pottstown Symphony. This name change initiative had also been championed and energetically supported by two recording companies, Cameo Classics in Europe and Newport Classic in the USA. Both had expressed interest in recording the Pottstown Symphony with its present music director. The quality of the orchestra had grown and the Philadelphia Inquirer had repeatedly praised the ensemble. Newport Classic had gone so far with these plans that, together with the music director and executive director, they were planning to record a multi-media version of Gustav Holst's masterwork, *The Planets*, using images from NASA's Hubble Telescope in an audiovisual extravaganza. This would have also been the first ever commercial recording for the Pottstown Symphony and it promised to the orchestra, through sales of DVDs and, mostly through downloads, a new source of significant income. The advantages to the orchestra in its fundraising and outreach programs, its education programs and the favorable impact on its bottom line were not to be denied. This could have

---

[141] Memo from Porter Eidam III to Executive Director dated 08 January 2008.
[142] Memo from board member and Chairman of the Name Change Committee to volunteer marketing expert dated 21 February 2008.

been the tool that would have given the orchestra the visibility and credibility it needed to climb out of its financial hole.

However, as with such projects, funding was necessary. Both record companies had also insisted that the name, "Pottstown Symphony" would not be one which would invite sales and encouraged the ensemble to make this change as quickly as possible. In fact, Newport Classic even offered its regular input into the change process and its decades-long marketing experience in such matters. After all, the recording company would also stand to lose were it to initiate the production of a product it could only sell with extreme difficulty. It was, in fact, exactly the name "Pottstown Symphony" that almost cost this orchestra the offer of a recording in the first place. The owner of Newport Classic and the executive director had been associates for many years and the executive director had sent him a recent recording of the orchestra in hopes of awakening interest in a recording project at some stage. Because of the name "Pottstown" he delayed for several months even listening to the recording until his wife reminded him that he owed the executive director a response, if only out of friendship. Only then did he realize the quality of the ensemble and of its conductor and proposed *The Planets* recording with the orchestra. Also, the owner of Cameo Classics, based in France, had let it be known to the executive director that he thought the name "Pottstown" to be somewhat "unfortunate".

The executive director engaged in an active fundraising program and, in short order, managed to collect $30,000 in contributions for the "Planets Project". The board did nothing while the musicians union dragged its feet in granting the necessary authorizations to even make the recording. The suspicion existed then, and still exists today, that the executive director of an orchestra in Reading may have been active in trying to prevent the Pottstown Symphony from achieving this milestone. This other orchestra was well connected with the AFM local in the Reading area and it had been reported that they were angry at the idea that Pottstown could have managed this coup where this older and financially more sound ensemble could not.

Eventually, the project died for reasons we will discuss in the next chapter but which also rest on the inability and unwillingness of the board to fundraise for what would have most likely proven to have been a triumph for the orchestra. In a memo of 04 March 2008, the executive director of the PSO wrote to the Pottstown Symphony Orchestra's labor attorney, Jeffrey Zimskind, who was representing the orchestra in a collective bargaining agreement negotiation: "Also, the AF of M has been dragging its collective feet on approving the recording project that it is now in danger of not happening. I may have lost the video editor for the recording and the recording company is asking me lots of questions."[143] The reply came quickly, sent by the newly-elected vice-president of the board: "Is this for real? Are we truly in danger of the *Planets* project not happening?"[144] There had been no assistance for this marketing initiative from this source or, for that matter from any other source within the board, and now that the project was in danger, it seemed a pale excuse for a board officer to express sorrow at the refusal of the board to provide the support it should have given freely and enthusiastically and which could have also provided some leverage to negotiate itself out of the dilemma caused by sudden and extra demands from the union which will be discussed later. A few days later, the project was cancelled. The $30,000 raised by the executive director were earmarked as restricted funds and had to be returned. There were no further offers of recording contracts made to the Pottstown Symphony.

Throughout all of this and despite the excellent attendance numbers at the Masterworks concerts and the Educational Outreach program which was performing to over 10,000 children each year, and despite the initiatives through Emmanuel Lutheran Church via the joint chamber music series and the activities which brought the handicapped, the poor and elderly into the concert hall, the board only complained at the poor results coming from any marketing initiatives. The complaints were loud and all seemed to come from the same source, a source that also refused to supply the financial bulwark the symphony needed to engage in anything but patchwork marketing and PR. The executive director and art director were using every possible and cost-free vehicle at their disposal and with no reliable budget to sustain any effort for any length of time. It was some of the more conservative and better positioned members of the board who, nevertheless, continued to adhere to past traditions as was shown in an analysis of the organization's strengths and weaknesses undertaken by the chairman of the new strategic planning committee, that among the key weaknesses of the organization were: "PR/Marketing effectiveness/poor advertising."[145] The ultimate misunderstandings of the roles of the executive team were uttered by the newly engaged recruit from the Business on Board group and future vice-president and, later, president of the organization during a board meeting sometime in 2008. His cynical comment to the executive director complaining about inadequate funding and the marketing possibilities contained in the *Planets* project for the orchestra and the potential income to be realized from this project was: "all you want to do is make concerts".

---

[143] Memo from Executive Director to Mr. Jeffrey Zimskind from 04 March 2008.
[144] Reply from Vice-President of the PSOA board to Executive Director dated 05 March 2008.
[145] 2008 SWOT Analysis prepared by PSOA Strategic Planning Committee.

There was no resistance to this comment. It showed, all too sadly, that this board understood nothing about the interactions which go into making a successful artistic institution.

It should also be remembered that the refusal of the board to support the "Mozart's Musical Cities" promotion, together with Collette Vacations and the regional travel agent most probably cost the symphony the respect of a portion of its stakeholders. It certainly cost them the continued support of the travel firm and created ill-will between the symphony and the representative of the tour provider. The unwillingness of the board to simply attend the presentation event and to show that the board was behind this action which, after all, was an effort with no risk and no cost to the symphony and which would have reaped the benefits of access to a new circle of patrons and donors, was a miserable failure of the organization to realize the impact of such initiatives on its, eventual, financial picture as well as on its overall public image.

If one were to reduce the analysis of these failed marketing efforts in Pottstown to their core issue, I believe that would be the inability of the organization to agree on its administrative, financial and other priorities. This should have been the first step taken by any, fledgling organization or any newly constituted strategic planning committee or executive committee. The senseless writing and re-writing of by-laws and the development of impeachment and other regulatory procedures should have been of secondary importance or, in fact, in many cases, of no importance at all to these groups. Most strongly, the attention of such a body to the effectiveness of its marketing and PR outreach should have begun with several, simple questions. Among these questions, the primary one should have been: "what is the ultimate goal of our marketing efforts?"

What was forgotten was the realization of the need for the organization to communicate at a basic level with its constituencies and stakeholders. Failing this basis, the symphony board could not agree among its governing and decision-making organs over which program or service changes it needed to make and it was helpless at developing alternative methods should these systems fail. Finally, the Pottstown Symphony was never united in recognizing and implementing either the short-term or the long-priorities for the organization. Given a supportive and active role of the board in fundraising, a situation which was not present in Pottstown, the engagement of a public relations firm or the search for one which would offer its services on an in-kind basis, might have been a solution. With the exception of the name change action and the volunteer involvement of the marketing expert from a regional chemical company, nothing along these lines was ever attempted.

Certainly the elements for a highly successful marketing of the Pottstown Symphony were present as early as late 2006. The awarding of the NEA grant gave the Pottstown Symphony Orchestra Association status among funders. The "season sponsorship" from the internationally operating medical systems company gave the orchestra a ranking among its other, sponsored organizations. Among these were the Bayreuth Festival in Germany, the Salzburg Festival in Austria and the Mozarteum Brasileira in São Paulo, Brazil. The awarding of a recording contract by Newport Classic gave the Pottstown Symphony an international and national visibility as well. No one can honestly say that these actions, all made possible by the staff and without board help, represent bad marketing. What was bad about the Pottstown Symphony Orchestra Association's marketing was the tacit refusal of the board to support any efforts undertaken by the staff on its behalf by simply providing a secure financial basis and more than lip-service support.

7. ZEBRAS

The Orchestra and its Musicians

At the end of its days, the relationships between the Pottstown Symphony and the musicians, represented by the American Federation of Musicians, were, at best, excessively strained. The reasons for this loss of confidence between the parties had much to do with the internal battles the organization was fighting and with the refusal of the board of the association to recognize that its role was as a governing organ and not as intermediary between the musicians and the music director.

It was far too late in this development, however, that certain members of the board began to realize that the meddling of several of their colleagues in the dichotomy separating the music director from her orchestra and the clandestine dialogues with individual musicians had created an incendiary personnel issue rather than be a response to any artistic concerns within the organization. As is the case in symphony orchestras, worldwide, the ultimate responsibility for the quality and quantity of the music performed and for the audience and general public's acceptance of that programming lies with the music director. The music director of the Pottstown Symphony was extraordinarily adept at creating programs of interest, in doing so within the ever narrowing financial limits imposed upon her by the growing deficit and in generating performances which, as has been reported in previous chapters, had won the attention and respect of internationally operating recording companies.

In this narrative, I have repeatedly reported on the inability of the board of the Pottstown Symphony to rid itself of the misconception that their major function was a social one. This misconception spread as well to the musicians with certain board members regularly initiating contact with individual musicians and engaging in private discussions with them regarding the music director and artistic policy. Early in this development, this practice led to board member led attacks on the music director and, later, also on the executive director, and to growing personnel difficulties within the orchestra. As is the case in every organization, there are persons whose "chemistry", cultural expectations or simple emotional makeup preclude anything approaching a warm and trusting relationship. This is always true in life and the circumstances are no different in a symphony orchestra where the role of the conductor and his or her authority dictate that the artistic head of such an ensemble receive and maintain absolute control over the artistic product. Rarely do audience members express their dissatisfaction over any orchestral concert by complaining about the person in the second row of violas or the individual performing on second bassoon. The causality for any complaints relative to an orchestral concert lies with the conductor and with his or her command of both the music and of the synchronous and artistic unity of the players who perform that music. An excellent oboist whom I know quite well once described the role of the conductor in such an ensemble as one of "herding cats". In this observation, he well summarized the situation in many orchestras, especially in per-service ones as was the Pottstown Symphony.

The culture of a per-service orchestra and the coordination of efforts in such an ensemble are made all that much more difficult by the nature of the employment practices used to fill the chairs. In the case of the Pottstown Symphony, the ensemble knew that, at some time, it would be confronted with genuine labor negotiations and would, eventually, be required to enter into a collective bargaining agreement with the musicians' union. However, the financial shortfall which restricted the symphony's flexibility for much of its existence also precluded any serious discussions about a time line for such an agreement. Increasingly the American Federation of Musicians was beginning to question the seriousness of the orchestra's intention to regionalize. After all, the fundraising was simply not happening and the debt was mounting and the complaints of no money for musicians and their salaries were becoming an almost eternal litany, to be heard from one season to the next. As a response, in 2005 the Pottstown Symphony, together with key musicians who regularly performed with the orchestra, created a membership agreement and grievance procedure and requested those who had been "grandfathered" on the personnel list for potential hires to vote on their acceptance of this process. It must be made clear here that the Reading local 135-211 of the American Federation of Musicians was party to the development of this document as was the Philadelphia local 77 of the AFM. There was no attempt, whatsoever, to mask any effort to avoid the eventual collective bargaining agreement via obtuse or otherwise convoluted regulations to the disadvantage of the musicians. In fact, both the union locals in Philadelphia and in Reading recognized, as did the music director, the personnel contractor and the manager of the orchestra and, later, also the newly hired executive director, that this mechanism would be a temporary measure until the symphony's board could wrest itself from its debt.

The procedures were quite simple. The orchestra recognized players as full members or associate members with a "Full Member" being a musician who had performed a simple majority of services during the previous three seasons. Any musician performing less than the majority of services during this period but who had performed more than three services per season was considered to be an "Associate Member". The "Full Members" were guaranteed their seating in the orchestra and the "Associate Members" would be hired as needed on a preferred basis but not guaranteed a certain position in the ensemble. Everyone else was considered a "Substitute" without guarantees of any kind.

The grievance procedure was equally straightforward. In case of grievances, usually of an artistic nature, between the music director and any musician, a meeting would be arranged by the personnel contractor in which the issue at hand would be negotiated among the music director and the personnel contractor with the musician in question. The personnel contractor would function as an intermediary in this process which was intended to lead to an understanding of the problem and to ways to reconcile it in the best interests of the musician, the music director and of the orchestra. There was also a second step to be taken in cases where this meeting produced no satisfactory result. In this second attempt at reconciliation, the music director, orchestra manager, personnel contractor and two of the musician's peers in the orchestra selected by the musician himself or herself would again review the matter and seek to negotiate a reasonable solution. Finally, were all these avenues to fail, the affected musician would be auditioned by the music director accompanied by three players from within the orchestra, each being principal performers on the same family of instruments as was the musician in question.

Even in this worst case, however, and assuming a decision against the performer, the music director would propose an alternative playing option that would also serve the needs of the orchestra. This could be a lower seating in the section for certain types of concerts or, in cases of an impasse, the loss of "Full Membership" and demotion to the status of "Associate Member".

In principle, there was nothing wrong with this procedure except that it had been implemented without, first, the music director having initiated the necessary and internal house cleaning required for it to properly function. Ideally, when the music director assumed her position in 2002, she would have used the first season to evaluate the body of players she had inherited and, in the following season, began the process of culling out those who did not or could not meet her expectations. For whatever reasons she may have had at that time, she decided, instead, to work with the performers who had been given to her and made no significant personnel changes within the orchestra. Clearly, this was a mistake in judgment on her part but one which would not show itself for several years to come. In the years 2002, 2003 and, perhaps also 2004, these personnel changes would have been relatively easy to make, assuming board support of the music director and trusting acceptance of her personnel decisions. If we disregard the social element and the fact that, at that time, several board members also performed as musicians in the Pottstown Symphony, the lack of any sort of binding employment agreements between the association and the musicians meant that anyone who performed with the PSO did so at the will of the music director. In order to avoid the issues of board/musician conflict of interest, it would have been necessary for the board of the Pottstown Symphony to have established the simple rule that no board member could also serve as a working musician in the orchestra and to leave the decision to the individuals involved whether they wanted to be musicians or management. Also this action, which could have easily been initiated in 2003 or 2004, would have avoided serious problems at a later time. With these two measures in place within the organization, the music director would have had a free hand with which to build the orchestra according to the model outlined by the board in its strategic plan and to do so without the cross-currents and conflicts which would later surface and which would involve a drama of intrigue involving the board, certain players, the labor union and rival orchestras in the region.

Up until the death of Porter Eidam, in 2000, the Pottstown Symphony had remained, for all intent and purposes, a local, community orchestra. Although the quality of the participating musicians had been steadily improved through Mr. Eidam's engaging of players from outside Pottstown, most notably from Philadelphia, there was still a "local" feeling about the orchestra and a drive from within the board to consistently show the organization's loyalty to the Pottstown community. At some time right before his death, the board had agreed with Mr. Eidam's position that the potential existed to create a regional orchestra from this core ensemble. In the years following the death of William Lamb, whose emphasis was more on school music, and the passing of Porter Eidam, who wished much more from this orchestra, the ensemble had quietly and significantly grown in the direction of professionalism. The problem here was, however, that the musical growth was not matched by the board growth and maturity and the presence of board members in the ensemble as performing musicians often created situations of conflict of interest.

One particular problem was the presence of the daughter of the presumed founder, herself a French horn player, and her interference in the musical conduct of the ensemble with the justification being her presumed role as carrier of the torch. In 2005 and 2006, she became involved in a conflict between the music director and a musician in the ensemble and used her self-appointed authority to conduct numerous conversations with this musician and as a launching pad for attacks in the board room targeted at the music director. This subject has been addressed in an earlier chapter but the ramifications of these attacks upon the music director and the knowledge gained by certain, less capable members of the orchestra who also enjoyed membership status, that they could circumvent the existing grievance procedures and go straight to a board member made it difficult to administer the artistic side of the organization.

In addition, the orchestral manager, the man who had already loaned $19,000 to the symphony, struggled at all costs to prevent any actions by the music director or, later, by the executive and music directors in tandem, that would have resulted in the music director enacting the grievance procedure against two players who belonged to his inner circle. At some point in the development of this orchestra following the death of Porter Eidam, it seemed as if the board and certain members of the administration had grown fearful of what a professionalization of this orchestra would really mean to their positions in the community. Many saw this as a loss of influence and of power which, done in a proper fashion, it would not have been. The orchestra manager became embroiled in convoluted arguments over what, exactly, constituted being a "Pottstowner" in the Pottstown Symphony. The arguments and defenses grew to such an absurd level that the executive director was compelled, in 2006, to defend the policy of hiring the best players by presenting to the board a chart of how many players as a whole came from which postal codes surrounding Pottstown. The simple truth that the development of a professional orchestra has nothing to do with the town in which one choses to live was ignored in favor of the position that this "professional" orchestra should only consist of Pottstown residents. The absurdity of this presumption in a town with a core population of 22,000 residents should be evident to any reader. However, this very absurd pretense also blatantly revealed the small town nature of this board and, had one looked closely enough at the problem, would also have begun to betray the roots of the xenophobia that was at work here.

With the breakdown of the grievance system and the presence of a growing problem created by certain "grandfathered" musicians who had begun to lose their ability to perform at the level desired and required by the music director, certain board members as well as the musician mentioned above began an initiative to oust the music director. The accusation was that in her conduct of the orchestra she was not "democratic" enough, that there was insufficient time given for which to "discuss" interpretations, and several other points which served to demonstrate the community orchestra thinking on the board. Yes, I am certain these actions were board member inspired. The risk in initiating these actions exposed the organization to great danger and potential breakdown of systems and the consequences were dramatic for the entire organization.

In 2006, when the newly elected but not yet officially recognized or sitting vice-president carried on his music director personnel evaluation at the behest of the former president of 20 years, this barrier between musicians and board had long been ruptured. Even though, in late 2005 or early 2006, in a meeting between the management of the Pottstown Symphony represented by the executive director, the music director, the personnel contractor and the orchestra manager and the Reading local 135-211 of the American Federation of Musicians and represented by its general secretary and its president, it was categorically agreed by all in attendance that the existing membership and grievance document would suffice until the Pottstown Symphony was financially able to support a collective bargaining agreement. This categorical agreement was soon forgotten by the union and, in early 2007, pressured by union officers from New York; the symphony was forced into catastrophic collective bargaining negotiations.

At least the orchestra manager, although he was both a member of the orchestra and sat on the board but did so without a vote, initially sided with the management team and with the music director. He was considered an associate member of the board of directors and, as such, functioned in an advisory capacity. However, increasingly he started to assume the position represented by the former president siding with the old guard on the board in their combined resistance to anything which spoke of change. There were two musicians in the orchestra, a flutist and an oboist, who with advancing age simply could not keep up with the increasing difficulties of the orchestra's expanding repertoire. Remember, the music director was fulfilling her mandate from the board and striving for a professional, regional orchestra and this meant for the players that the technical level of each of them had to rise to the difficulties to be found in the repertoire selected for this and coming seasons. The music director sought a solution where these two players could continue their relationship with the Pottstown Symphony but on a level where they would not be a disadvantage to the quality the ensemble was striving for in its Masterworks concerts. Others from outside the region came into play in this mini drama since one of the musicians in question, a flutist, was also the spouse of an executive at a rival orchestra. It was, in fact, the orchestra manager and associate board member who maintained that all must remain loyal to the Pottstown Symphony's identity as determined by the presumed founding father while he, himself, lived in another town, many miles away from Pottstown and also performed in the same orchestra where the flutist's husband was an executive on the management team. It was a case of a double standard being applied in order to rescue the status quo. He and the others were simply afraid of change. The ultimate resolution of this issue was suggested by the personnel contractor and accepted by the music director and was, in and of itself, in keeping with the socially conscious nature of the entire grievance formulation. The two players were allowed to retain their "Membership" status but would perform only in the pops concerts and in other concerts where the repertoire was less demanding. No one would have lost face here but the orchestra manager saw even this solution as an affront and submitted his resignation from the ensemble, maintaining that the Pottstown Symphony had somehow been irreparably damaged by the music director's replacing of two players with reduced abilities and only for certain concerts. The absurdity in this position and the fundamental immaturity it showed brought chaos into the organization which was made worse by the board's refusal or inability to simply accept this man's resignation and get on with it! Remember the Pottstown Symphony Orchestra Association still owed him $19,000 at this point and he had started to use this debt as leverage to blackmail the organization and attempt to blackmail the music director.

In late 2006, as the New York headquarters of the American Federation of Musicians increased its pressure on the symphony to agree to collective bargaining, the board member who had been the association's grant writer before the entrée of the executive director onto the scene continued to fill her seat as well as a seat in the orchestra, among those in the rear row of cellists. In winter, 2007, the owner of the audio postproduction firm from Philadelphia, the same man who had recommended the orchestra consider insolvency, prepared at his own expense multiple copies of a recent performance of Berlioz's *Symphonie fantastique* and distributed this recording with the Pottstown Symphony to each of the board members. The purpose was to inspire them to use the quality of this performance as a way to jump-start their fundraising and give them something to show as proof of what was happening there. It was on this day that this board member and cellist finally left the board room, saying little, and leaving the newly minted CDs behind. On the one hand, she had clearly decided that her loyalty would remain with the musicians while, on the other, she was also happy enjoying her role as a board member just so long as no demands were made on her through this position. This time, however, when she would have had to have been active in one role or another, she clearly abrogated her responsibilities as a member of the board. Evidently, fundraising in this context, with no compensation should she prove to have been successful, would have compromised her in some way. When the AFM began its action against the symphony, in late 2006, this same woman had gladly assumed the role as mole on the board serving in the interests of the union organizing committee much as she had violated her obligations to the organization's financial health on another occasion. Up to her departure in 2007, she had attended both board meetings and union organization meetings. The symphony had, on one occasion and in an attempt to clarify its position, called a post rehearsal meeting of the orchestral musicians. The members of the organizing committee attended (a privilege not afforded to the symphony management when it came to explanations from the organizers) and this still-board-member showed her combined loyalty and disloyalty by firmly taking a seat in the front row alongside the head of the organizing committee, the musician who had initiated this action in her early discussions with the daughter of the presumed founder of the orchestra.

The circumstances surrounding this attempt at forcing a collective bargaining agreement on the orchestra have their roots in the concerns of the board and certain of its members that the music director was taking too much public attention away from them and focusing it on the artistic evolution of the Pottstown Symphony. As I have repeatedly stated, this began with the frontal attacks on the music director at board meetings and segued into private discussions between certain board members and others in the orchestra who were opposed to this music director. The problem was that her standards were high. They had to be so to achieve the goals the board had determined it wanted of her. However, this high standard also required that each member of this orchestra be in the position to perform at the level demanded of him or her. What made this pressure worse was the permanent financial crisis which reduced the number of affordable rehearsals to a minimum. There was no room for discussion or debate and the problem of hiring a per-service orchestra where the organization maintained loyalty to the musicians through the membership agreement but the musicians were not bound to the ensemble in any way except their wish (or not so) to remain a member in good standing, meant that the hiring of personnel for each and every concert was an adventure in and of itself.

The music director survey was the most blatant and banal attack on the organization's artistic leader and its failure to achieve her dismissal, demotion or simply personal degradation and her submission to the reduced norms certain members of the board were striving to clandestinely establish, led to the next step in this process which was an attack on the orchestra by some of its musician members.

The pay scale for the Pottstown Symphony had never been overly generous. However, it had been fair in consideration of the financial pressures on the association and remained within the norms approved by the American Federation of Musicians locals in the region. Also, both the music director and the executive director had clearly expressed their belief that a collective bargaining agreement with the musicians in the Pottstown Symphony was a goal to strive for and both had done so to the Reading local as well as to local 77 in Philadelphia. It was absolutely no secret that, in the opinion of the management team, the only obstacle to the establishment of a collective bargaining agreement with the American Federation of Musicians was a financial one which was out of the hands of the music and executive directors to resolve. What made this organizational effort all the more sinister was the assertion by many on the organizing committee that "as many of you might recall, although the [executive director] openly stated in the October 2006 management meeting that he was in full support of the card count, what followed was a string of delay tactics that ultimately prevented the card count from being carried out. We hope that, since some progress has been made in this area in his absence [six months], [he] will no longer impede the process now under way."[146]

In fact, the executive director had in no way impeded this card count which was designed to determine which of the qualifying musicians in the ensemble stood behind this collective unionization. What was going on instead was a plea to both local 135-211 and local 77 to simply respect the conditions reflected in the membership agreement which had been agreed to a year earlier and which was supposed to act as a quasi-collective bargaining document until such time as the orchestra could carry the weight of a full union contract. Furthermore, musicians within the ensemble itself, most notably the personnel contractor who was also the bass trombone player in the orchestra, complained that the voting cards sent to the musicians were designed to mislead them and stated that this vote, in his interpretation, "was an endorsement that we be represented by the union but that the return of the card endorsed a CBA."[147] His question was a basic one which was ignored by the organizing committee in a blitz attack on him and on the organization but, most especially, on the management team. His basic question, which went unanswered, was: "Which is it? Are we voting that we be union members or are we endorsing a CBA? If non-union members are correct that the orchestra cannot require union membership under PA law what are these cards all about?"[148]

An increasingly rancorous and dissenting trail of discussions issued from this exchange involving, as well, the introduction of a labor lawyer and union expert who, *pro bono*, agreed to represent the Pottstown Symphony

---

[146] Memo from the Organizing Committee of the Pottstown Symphony to performing musicians dated 19 July 2007.
[147] Memo from Pottstown Symphony Personnel Contractor and Bass Trombonist from 2006. Exact date unknown.
[148] Ibid.

Orchestra Association against this attack on its existence. The singular unfairness of these procedures is demonstrated by the refusal of the organizing committee and of the American Federation of Musicians to allow the bass trombonist, a card carrying member of several locals including 135-211 and local 77, to attend any of its meetings on the grounds that, as personnel contractor for the orchestra, he was considered to be management while, at the same time, welcoming the cellist who had leaked information to the union and who, it is believed, was still a board member at this time. This amounted to an essential disenfranchisement of the bass trombonist on the part of his own labor representatives. It is to be noted here that as personnel contractor, he acted under instructions from the music director and, as such, had little executive authority while the cellist and board member operated at the highest level of decision making power in the organization.

In March, 2008, there was an initial meeting between the union committee and officers of the American Federation of Musicians on one hand and the association's labor attorney, the executive director and with the presence of the newly elected vice-president, the drama teacher, on the other. The organizing committee presented a document to the orchestra that clearly exceeded the ability of the symphony to meet the demands contained therein. While denying the presumption it had long represented that it be involved in artistic and business policy, it simultaneously demanded representation on the Pottstown Symphony board and on all PSOA board committees. This representation would have continued the one-way flow of information, much of it sensitive, from the board room directly to the union without guaranteeing to the Pottstown Symphony management the same privilege in return.

Financially, this agreement, especially in light of the deficit picture which, as you may remember had developed so far that in February the internal auditor and board member and the executive director had advised considering bankruptcy and in March the Nonprofit Finance Fund had stressed the hopelessness of the situation in a detailed report, paid no attention to the same financial crisis which had prompted the letter of 12 February 2007 demanding that the Pottstown Symphony provide an escrow account to guarantee payment to its musicians. The proposed collective bargaining agreement demanded increases in travel allotments, attempted to limit the number of copies of archival recordings the organization could reproduce for grant and funding applications, and required an across-the-board per-service pay increase. Although these organizers were quite aware of the catastrophic financial picture in the Pottstown Symphony, they were willing to forget reality and try and force through a document that would, certainly, have guaranteed them permanent unemployment from this organization. From this distance, it is my opinion that the attacks on the music director and, through this collective bargaining agreement document on the orchestra itself and its existence, were nothing less than a form of terrorism by the few to the crass disadvantage of the many. Primary clauses in the collective bargaining agreement were also included to force membership in the Reading local 135-211 as well as a pension contribution from the orchestra which, as was clear to all concerned, would have been an impossible financial hurdle for the Pottstown Symphony to overcome.

Returning to the initial meeting between the management of the Pottstown Symphony and the leadership of the Reading local in 2006 and to the then agreement of the American Federation of Musicians that the membership and grievance document was equivalent to a preliminary collective bargaining agreement, it is important to note that the Pottstown Symphony, up until this organizing action, was a committed advocate of union membership for its musicians and had, in fact, instituted the practice of only hiring musicians with a union card. In addition, prior to the attack by the organizing committee on the orchestra and its music director, the Pottstown Symphony had been praised by local 135-211 for, exactly, this policy.

Finally, the organizing committee tried in this document to impede the right of the music director to adjust the seating in the orchestra in an attempt to guarantee the positions of those on that very committee. It is to be noted here that several of those represented on this committee were also players exhibiting significant technical and ensemble difficulties and whom the music director would gladly have replaced had the situation been somewhat different and had she received the expected and unequivocal backing of the board in such a decision. Because certain of the board members had also played a political game as moles in the interests of the union and as interlocutory with certain musicians, the unbridled support the music director should have received and which she had rightfully and justifiably earned, was never forthcoming.

Whatever happened to this drive to collectivize the Pottstown Symphony after spring 2008 is unknown. For a while, there were reports that the union organizing committee had been working with the board to help restructure the organization following the departure of much of the board and all of the executive team. In February 2009, the former orchestra personnel contractor, who continued to act as bass trombonist for the orchestra, was suddenly demoted from a principal player to a sectional one with comparable per-service pay reduction. Many saw this as a revenge action since he supported the reform drive within the orchestra and defended the continued viability of the still-existing grievance document. At that point, in early March 2009, he resigned from the Pottstown Symphony. This decision to demote him had ostensibly been made by the drama teacher who was by now the new and third president of the board and conveyed by the newly hired personnel contractor who, interestingly enough, was also connected with the outside orchestra whose executive was married to the flutist whom the music director in Pottstown needed to remove from certain concerts. The bass trombone player in his role as personnel contractor had also endorsed this quality dictated and urgently needed change in personnel. A year later, the personnel contractor who delivered this message to the bass trombonist also found herself no longer working for the Pottstown Symphony.

Most sinister of all, however, was the role of the American Federation of Musicians and of Local 135-211 in the approval process for the Pottstown Symphony's proposed recording of *The Planets* which would have been released by the US label, Newport Classic, and which stood an excellent chance of dramatically improving the symphony's financial picture. At the point where the production had been agreed to between the orchestra and the recording company, the Pottstown Symphony management immediately contacted the Reading local of the AFM to secure the approval for the participation of union musicians in a commercial recording project. There were those on the Pottstown board who immediately began asking how soon they could get out of the project, if they needed to do so, and no one on the Pottstown Symphony board raised any money for the recording, except the executive director and music director. Either the relationship between Local 135-211 and an outside orchestra was so close, that the local continually dragged its feet in issuing any authorizations to the symphony for the recording or that the management of Local 135-211 was so incompetent or afraid of the reaction from the New York headquarters that it had no idea whether to approve, reject or stonewall the initiative. The CBA action was in full swing at this stage but the completion of this recording project contained nothing in its conditions that would have gone against any possible or probable terms contained in any future collective bargaining agreement. The executive director in Pottstown waited weeks for a reply from the American Federation of Musicians and, finally, after writing to Local 135-211 several times, contacted the head of the Philadelphia Local 77, asking if he could intercede at the national level. Again, this appeal proceeded at a snail's pace, if there had been any movement in it at all, and the Pottstown Symphony was getting bombarded by questions from the record company asking why the mill was grinding so slowly. Following a further telephone conversation between the executive director and Local 77, the executive director received a phone call at his home from a representative of the American Federation of Musicians in Los Angeles. The content of this conversation had no other effect but to destroy the hopes of the Pottstown Symphony that its recording of *The Planets* could ever be realized. The voice on the other end, the representative for the union, simply said that he would offer the Pottstown Symphony a special deal for the union OK for this project. The orchestra association would have to pay the AFM the ridiculous amount of $45,000 at which point the union would grant a green light for the recording. To the question: "if we do that, what should I pay the musicians?" the reply was: "I don't care". Clearly, this demand from the AFM was nothing more than an attempt to wrest money from the orchestra that, as was known to both locals, the orchestra didn't have. It should be noted here that the package the Pottstown Symphony was offering to the players included not only a higher per-service rate for the sessions but also a royalty percentage. If this project were to become as successful as all had hoped and expected it would have been, the musicians would have profited handsomely from the production. However, this was of no interest to their union. I stop short of calling this action a blatant exercise in graft. However, it is clear here that the future of the musicians in its trust played no role in the union's decisions governing this project. Shortly thereafter, the recording died, driven to its death by the inflexibility of the AFM, the failure and refusal of the board to fund-raise and by an incredible degree of jealousy and small-mindedness from musicians and colleagues in the region.

Whatever good might have come from the involvement of a labor union in this story was clearly eliminated by the behavior of the national organization of the American Federation of Musicians, the two locals in the immediate area and a small handful of technically and musically inadequate players who were interested in nothing else than in preserving their jobs, even if in doing so the organization that engaged them went bankrupt. I cannot imagine what they must have thought or, in fact, if they had thought at all. The rivalry of the "other" orchestra in the region is easy to fathom. The Pottstown Symphony was getting too important, too "big for its britches", and there was too little room on the "range" for two organizations of approximately equal caliber. It was enough that the Philadelphia Orchestra was 40 miles away and, if one were adventurous enough, one could also enjoy the excellent orchestras in Allentown or in Scranton. Fifteen miles was simply too close for this sort of rivalry and, well, the cowboys west of Pottstown had started circling the wagons.

8. THE LAST YEAR

"Le Prince d'Aquitaine à la tour abolie"[149]

In his study on the role of politics and economics in a democratic culture, Lambert Zuidervaart writes of the conflict art and culture generate in the discussion "between art as liberating transgression and art as a decadent menace. Built into such polarities are individualistic assumptions about artists and their publics and vanguardist assumptions about the role of arts in society."[150]

In Pottstown, in the final years of the symphony's existence, this very existential question was at the core of the organization's dissolution. Especially at the end of this story, there were factors from within the board that had determined the only way to "rescue" the symphony was to destroy it in order to rid their organization of the specter of unwanted and often foreign ideas. These initiatives seem to have begun at the end of 2006 with the music director survey, a topic already discussed here, and continued into 2007 with the statement by the former board president at a cloistered board retreat that this would be the final chance the board had to "do something" about the music director and executive director. By not assuming this challenge to simply fire the two employees, the battle for control of the Pottstown Symphony entered a further and, this time, Pyrrhic phase.

An example of this draconic strategy was the reported and clandestine discussions between a rival orchestra and the delegated representative of a local superintendent of schools who was also the former board president and originator of the last ditch effort at the board member retreat to rid the Pottstown Symphony of its executive team. It was reported to the Pottstown Symphony's personnel contractor by a musician in this rival orchestra that the school district under the control of the former board president had contacted another and smaller orchestra, located a few miles from Pottstown, with the proposal that this orchestra could wrest a portion of the agreement for the educational concerts in that district from the Pottstown Symphony. It must be made clear here that these "Educational Outreach Concerts" were an important factor for the symphony which also helped to establish a certain, however fragile, degree of financial stability. They were

---

[149] T.S. Eliot: *The Waste Land - What the Thunder Said.* "Le Prince d'Aquitaine à la tour abolie": Eliot's note: V. Gerard de Nerval, sonnet El Desdichado. The title means "The Disinherited"; the line, "The Prince of Aquitaine at the ruined tower."Faber and Faber Ltd., London, 1940 & 1972.

[150] Lambert Zuidervaart: *Art in Public.* Cambridge University Press, New York, 2011. page 208.

also concerts, performed repeatedly at several school districts in the region, which served a school-age audience of about 10,000 children, their teachers and the school administration. The concept was multi-media and multi-discipline and promoted partnerships with other arts organizations, especially with an excellent regional ballet company. Together with the director of this ballet company, the music director of the Pottstown Symphony had developed a concept that proved to be flexible, entertaining and, for the Pottstown Symphony, also profitable. As the program grew, it began to also acquire legendary status in the region and many of the participating school districts and most of the students and their teachers eagerly awaited the next round of performances.

In the winter of 2008, this report of a planned pillaging of these performances and the role of the former board president in this intrigue had become known to the music director. She and the personnel contractor told the executive director of this plan and the three of them brought it up at the next board meeting. At first, there didn't seem to be much surprise from several of the board members, except at learning that the management team also knew of the plot. The board president and wife of the headmaster expressed her doubts at the truth of this report from the music director and executive director. Others among the board officers, many of whom had been appointed to the board by the superintendent of schools and former board president whose loyalty was finally being called to question, turned the question into an attack on the employees who, in their whistle-blowing were only interested in rescuing something of importance to the symphony's survival. The response from the board president and the board officers was, simply, their reluctant agreement to ask the now accused and former board president if there was any truth to this accusation. If you as reader of this story will remember the impeachment procedure previously levied against a sitting board member for simply expressing his opinion, it becomes even more compelling in this context since there was no thought or discussion given to any form of disciplinary action should the accusation have proven itself to have been true. Also, the idea that the accused would be asked if she had done anything wrong or initiated any action to cause this to have happened was clearly nothing more than a smoke screen, Pottstown style.

At the following board meeting, a month later, it was reported that she had, indeed, been asked but that the reply was that she had done nothing. However, these accusations kept reappearing, coming from other musicians and others in the know in the region and it was clear that there was some substance to this charge. Whether the assignment had been given to an underling to explore this possibility or whether the exploration had been undertaken in a sort of lone-wolf action by an employee of the school district wishing to make points with the superintendent and the school board, is something no one will ever know except those who spearheaded this inquiry. What is interesting about this, however, is the later development which led to the agreed-to concerts ultimately not being performed in this district.

Despite what was a growing body of circumstantial evidence that, in fact, there was substance to the accusation made by the music director and executive director, the board did nothing to guarantee that the school district in question live up to its long existing commitment to the symphony for concerts the following April. The tale of the misinformation given to the executive director and music director by the board's assistant treasurer in which he misrepresented the symphony's available cash with which to pay the musicians and other costs for these concerts was exacerbated by the sudden news, delivered only days before the scheduled performance and at a time when the entire orchestra had been engaged and the organization had made a financial commitment to the musicians, that exactly these concerts scheduled for this one and now problematic school district had been summarily cancelled by the district and that no damages of any kind would be paid by the district to the symphony as a result of this abrupt and last minute cancellation. This begs the question of the lack of a proactive role that had been played by the symphony's attorney who, in fulfilling this function, should have advised the board of this possibility at some time in its future and should have generated a binding agreement between the symphony and the various school districts for their participation in the Educational Outreach Concerts. This agreement would also have had to include a penalty clause in case of withdrawal after a certain date. Once again, the lack of commitment by this organization to itself and its failure to protect itself from potential harm resulted in damage to the institution. The last minute withdrawal of this school district left a gaping hole in the Pottstown Symphony's performance schedule. With a series of nine concerts to be played, all within three days, the placement of this cancellation on the second day of the concert run, a placement previously agreed to between the orchestra and the school district in question, meant that the Pottstown Symphony Orchestra Association was now obligated to pay the musicians for this idle day if it expected to retain their services for the entire period. It also meant that the income expected from these nine concerts would be reduced by about one-third which consequently led to a nominally profitable series of concerts netting a loss for the organization. The damage was total and there was little anyone could do or was ready to do to seek reparations from the school district which had caused the problem. It is important to note that this district also belonged to one of the wealthiest in the region and that such an abrupt cancellation would not have been caused by a financial shortfall there. It was clear to many that the genuine reason for this cancellation was an effort to drive out the two hated employees by simply driving the orchestra into ruin. The board of the Pottstown Symphony had become a suicide commando and there were those within the organization who would rather see the organization die than allow it to be led, administratively and musically, in a progressive and, up to now, quite successful manner. The progressive staff leadership had, up to now, generated synergetic relationships with senior citizens institutions, with the Montgomery County Association for the Blind as well as with Emmanuel Lutheran Church, it had generated a customer-friendly ticketing system that was immediately accepted by the public and resulted in increased attendance. In addition, this same management team had established working relationships with two important record companies, with an international tour operator and with the extra-regional press. Finally, this same team had broken through the difficult funding barrier and secured a financial booster from the National Endowment and promises from the William Penn Foundation as well as created a friendly, professional and productive relationship with the season sponsor. In short, it seemed that all elements for a productive and successful future for the Pottstown Symphony were in place. As far as its competence and ability to speak for the organization and to create business relationships between the symphony and outside partners was concerned, the executive team had opened doors for the board to pass through. What were needed were only the support of the board for these efforts and a stable financial condition within the organization.

This accusation that the board of the Pottstown Symphony had begun to act like a cadre of suicide bombers was supported by a discussion between the music director and the insurance broker who was also a member of the board. The music director asked her if it was the intent of some on the board to "tank the organization". She received no answer but the person questioned lowered her head and replied with body language as if to acquiesce. What I must now describe as irrational hatred of the management team seems to have infected the psyche of some on this board of directors.

Before this incident had peaked to where it exacerbated an already serious financial and moral crisis, however, others of the board members had resolved that they would take action to stop this downward spiral and seek a sweeping internal housecleaning. The impetus of this was the report of the internal auditor of the orchestra's season sponsor along with the report of the executive director. Both parties had recommended bankruptcy. In March, following discussions the previous January with the independent attorney in Valley Forge, a growing number of board members, supported by all but one of the employees, had agreed that the time had come to demand that this entire board be pressured to resign. Among those agreeing to this dramatic step were the internal auditor, and one of the bankers in question who was also a major creditor of the symphony, the art director and advertising executive who was also a board member and several others. It seemed at this stage that a slight majority of those on the board were in favor of change. The executive director and music director, associate board members without a vote but also those most affected by the continuing board irresponsibility, stood behind this putsch as did the personnel contractor and, yes, even the symphony's administrative assistant seemed supportive of the action, even though she would have and could have played no role in its implementation.

After many meetings, discussions and strategy sessions, the rebellious members of the board determined among themselves that they would force an emergency board meeting for a few days hence. The timing was critical to them since their majority was quite narrow and one member of this group was leaving for his vacation in a few days. In essence, they had less than a week to meet and to agree among themselves on a strategy which they would then implement a day or two later. It had been shown, time and again, that any parliamentary efforts to reform or correct the dangerous course the Pottstown Symphony Orchestra Association had been following these past decades had failed, crashing on the rocks of internal politics and intra-social dependencies. On those occasions where the board as a unit would agree to something which was not approved of by its officers or that flew in the face of its expectations of gain for the few at the expense of the many, a subsequent board meeting would be held in the parking lot on the same night, attended by only the few who met to sabotage the decision of the majority. The decisions made in those clandestine parking lot meetings were the real face of the board of this orchestra. By the time the rebels within the ranks had been driven to rise up and fight for the further existence of the orchestra, any sense of democratic principles and fair-play had long been lost to a deeper need to hold on to authority. In a political sense, the Pottstown Symphony had become a musical and artistic banana republic.

In a memo sent on Sunday, 23 March 2008 to the leader and organizer of this initiative to rescue the orchestra from itself, the executive director wrote the following: "The crisis in which we and the PSOA find ourselves is one not caused by individuals but by the synergetic impact of a group which, through its mob mentality and inappropriate business decisions based either on personal comfort levels or on simple lack of knowledge, have driven the organization to the point of insolvency. In the process of arriving at this point, they have placed the lives and careers of the employees and their families at risk, potentially and irreparably damaged the reputation of the association, and created internal systems which have resulted in a rift within the board itself."[151]

From the very beginning, the executive director had cautioned those on the board who were trying to wrest power from the status quo that they would need to forget that they were gentlemen and to approach their demands with a stringency and brutality that equaled that of those they were seeking to unseat. It was the opinion of the executive director, one also shared by the music director, that an extraordinary hardness was required if this action was to have any chance of success. Alas, this position was not universally supported by all of those who made up the group of reformers.

On the day before the emergency board meeting that had been called by the leader of the reform movement demanding change, both the music director and the executive director received telephone calls at home asking them to, once again, confirm what they had already promised in writing, i.e. if this action were to fail that they would immediately submit their resignations. This they confirmed in separate calls from the banker and creditor with several of the group serving as witness on these conference calls.

On the next day, at the suddenly called emergency board meeting, the rancor and parliamentary maneuvering of the old guard succeeded in defeating the motion to dissolve the body. Additional meetings were held between the board president and the banker and others, all without result. The old board remained in power and the newly formed, reform organization was fast losing its internal solidarity and its courage.

There was one last effort made with the executive director confronting the board president and, in the name of the organization, demanding her resignation. He documented her incredible incompetency and outlined to her the systems under which the organization would or could continue. Because it would have been necessary for the entire board to terminate itself as a body, that would have made of the executive director the new, temporary and interim board head. It would have been his responsibility to assemble a new board of directors, consisting of financial supporters and business people with ideas and resources to rid the Pottstown Symphony of its suffocating burden of indebtedness. The board president balked at this idea. It flew in the face of her elitist position that only one of those chosen could serve. Her private school background and sense of privileged position in society prevented her from realizing that the rescue of the Pottstown

---

[151] Memo dated 23 March 2008 from Executive Director of the Pottstown Symphony to select board members, the Music Director and head of the reorganization drive within the association.

Symphony was simply a matter of business experience, ideas and the willingness to allow some dirt to get under one's fingernails. Clearly she had seen herself as a member of the chosen elite. In this circumstance, however, with the orchestra facing ruin, there was no room left for this flawed concept of self-importance.

The board president protested that she would need to get a vote of the board for such an action, something that had already been tried and had failed. The executive director agreed to give her a few days for this action, something he also should not have done since those days were exactly what she and the others needed to put together an effective resistance strategy. At the end, the executive director also proved to be too weak to force any movement or change or, in fact, the simple admission by the board president and other of the organization's officers that change was even necessary.

It was now mid-April, 2008. The meetings had been held and the private and committee discussions had all happened and there was no result. Nothing had changed, nothing would change and there was no more room in this drama for discussion regarding change of any kind.

Demoralized and realizing that there was no recourse for them but to terminate their relationships with the Pottstown Symphony or risk personal and career ruin, the members of the what I would now call this "rescue action" met in a restaurant in Pottstown to decide their last move. They determined, unanimously, to hold to their initial threat to resign if no change was forthcoming and proffered their immediate resignations from the organization. This suggestion was agreed upon, unanimously, and the letters of resignation were written and prepared for submission to the board president.

What had brought this tragedy to this point was the betrayal of the banker and holder of the PSOA's note and line of credit to the special interests represented by the sitting board officers. This man had been at the forefront of the action to rescue the symphony. He had often been put under pressure by his bank to call in the loan the symphony held and with which there was little movement towards repayment. The best he could do was to refuse to renew the symphony's $10,000 line of credit, even though there was some motion afoot to try and repay this at some time. His concerns, however, had not been entirely financial. His wife was dying of cancer and one of her last pleas to him was that he would use his position and influence in the community to save the Pottstown Symphony. He knew that the collateral the bank had accepted to guarantee these loans, the orchestra's music library that had been offered to the bank with the assurance that it had a value of many tens-of-thousands-of dollars, was either offered with an overestimation of its worth or the board's maintaining this to be the true value was a downright lie. The executive director had brought this to his attention in a discussion where the bank manager had tried to comfort the ED's concerns by telling him that the symphony's officers had assured him of this high replacement value. Initially, he had refused to believe the executive director but the confirmation of this deception by an executive of a major music distributor in the region, only served to confirm that, in fact, these large loans were, in effect, unsecured ones.

One cannot know what external pressures had been put on this banker to betray those to whom he had allied himself. What is clear, however, is that in the last meeting where the demand for the board resignations was openly brought to protocol, he showed his true stripes and defected to the position of the hardline, Pottstown guard. He had become the symphony's quisling. The battle had been lost and, now, it became a matter of those who had given and risked so much to preserve this organization to simply walk away from it.

The music director wrote: "Due to the chronic fiduciary, fiscal and moral irresponsibility exhibited by the majority of the directors of the Pottstown Symphony Orchestra Association."[152] The position of the executive director was somewhat sterner but the message was the same: "I have watched and struggled against the chronic incompetence exhibited by much of the board of directors and its officers and I have battled against your immoral neglect of your obligations to the region and to your employees, and have witnessed among you denial, arrogance and hostility on a massive scale."[153]

Other letters, not quite as dramatic in their tone, were submitted by four board members one of them being the representative of the pharmaceutical products company that supplied the symphony its season sponsorship, and by the personnel contractor. The Pottstown Symphony as an organization had been reduced to a wasteland with no operative and experienced employees willing any longer to associate themselves with the association. The season sponsor refused to renew his sizable contribution and the pleas of the remaining board to reconsider this decision were met with the reply by the company's marketing vice-president that they, a multinational corporation which could have secured the financial future of the symphony for years to come had the board of the symphony simply acknowledged its obligations and acted upon them, would not even consider reopening discussions with the Pottstown Symphony over funding, either then or in the long-term future.

---

[152] Music Director resignation letter of 22 April 2008.
[153] Executive Director resignation letter of 22 April 2008.

A month later, as the news became known in the region, the former board president who had tried so hard and for so long to eliminate the organization from the unholy influence of the music and executive directors lauded the musicians in her glee at what had recently taken place. At this stage, the subjective nature of the Pottstown Symphony's history and the myth of its creation completed the circle of misinformation. The legend was now complete. She wrote: "Please think carefully about Bill Lamb and Porter Eidam and their devotion to this orchestra before you make a decision that you may regret. Whatever your decision, please remember that many of us are so grateful to you for all you have given for this orchestra. Without all of you, we would have never reached the pinnacle that we were able to attain."
[154] The personnel contractor, who had resigned this position but remained with the orchestra as its bass trombone player, was not on the distribution for this email. Also, the still active, but behind the scenes, orchestra manager who had fought any change of any kind, no matter how slight and no matter what the consequences of his action would have meant to the future of the ensemble, remained loyal to the still remaining board members. It is to be remembered as well that, at this point in the story, the board had, somehow, managed to repay to him the sum of $19,000 which had been loaned to the organization, with interest, many years before. In the Pottstown Symphony's IRS forms 990 from 26 August 2009 and 990-EZ from 03 March 2010, outstanding loans amounting to a total of $27,500 appear as part of the tax returns.[155] On the tax return submitted in 2010, the rationale for these loans has been given as "operating cash flow".[156] From this statement alone, it is clear that the Pottstown Symphony was operating under the social pressure not to fail. Also, the organization was standing under the spotlight of litigation which would have prevented its declaring insolvency before that matter had been settled.

In the chapter on personnel issues and the musicians, I discussed the issue of two members of the orchestra who were now beyond their prime and who needed to be put into a position where the orchestra could develop without them. At that time, I wrote of the resistance of these musicians to their demotion and of the stonewalling of the orchestra manager in any cases where his friends or friends of others in his circle would be adversely affected by the implementation of such a decision. What I did not state at that point was the peculiar situation within the Pottstown Symphony, and one which

---

[154] Memo from former Board President (of 20 years) to the musicians in the Pottstown Symphony Orchestra dated 18 May 2008.
[155] Pottstown Symphony Orchestra Association submitted IRS Form 990 from 26 August 2009 and IRS Form 990-EZ from 03 March 2010. Source GuideStar.org.
[156] Ibid.

further displays the amateurishness of this board that allowed the symphony's URL[157] and ownership of its domain name to become the property of the orchestra manager instead of that of the Pottstown Symphony Orchestra Association. This begs the question as to what serious business would risk leaving the future of its web presence to the whims and loyalty of a private individual. Redirecting his loyalty, this orchestra manager first resigned his position but, for reasons that remain vague even today, the board refused to act on his resignation. One can only presume the intrigue that went on behind the scenes and imagine the threats from both sides were he to be confirmed in his stated intention to leave the orchestra. He joined forces with the union organizing committee, however, maintaining his position as, in first instance, a "musician" and occasionally made a guest appearance at Pottstown Symphony board meetings where, as still an employee in good standing, he was entitled to take his place as a non-voting associate director. Along with the already described board member and one-time fundraiser who had also sided with the organizing committee against the interests of the orchestra, these two created a source of insider information, assisted by leaks from others on the board, which went straight from the board room to the union.

On 18 May 2008, this sometimes-on, sometimes-off board member sent the following email to what proves, in retrospect, to have been a unique list of recipients. He said: "Believe it or not, I have not submitted my resignation yet, either. I have mixed feelings and have been on leave of absence since February of 2007. This week a board member left messages on my voice-mail but I have not had time to return her call yet…Many of us have been spiritually or musically abused in various ways and feel exhausted, but we need to consider this question: Will we allow a handful of people to destroy this orchestra?…We need to know if there are enough current and future board members who share this same commitment. If so, this orchestra will not only survive, but it can grow in different ways beyond the imaginations of the former music director and former executive director, This orchestra is much more than another conductor and a suit who worked for Sony a very long time ago."[158]

It was clear what side of the fence this man stood on and, more importantly, his politics and the compass of the intrigue that had been going on these past years was made evident through the list of those to whom he sent this

---

[157] Uniform Resource Locator is a specific character string that constitutes a reference to a web site.
[158] Memo of the former Orchestra Manager of the Pottstown Symphony to members of the orchestra, board and other interested and involved persons dated 18 May 2008.

message. Among them were not only all those on the union organizing committee but also the New York based American Federation of Musicians negotiator, the AFM official in New York who had organized this railroading of the orchestra into contract negotiations at a time most precarious for the orchestra's existence, the president and vice-president of the board, the still serving executive director of the rival orchestra where, it is and was assumed, he had plotted to help overturn the *Planets* recording only a few months before and the Pottstown Symphony's concert master. The concert master had, on one hand, pledged his support for the action to reform the organization. He had been present at several meetings where the deficiencies of the board and the need for change had been discussed and agreed upon and had pledged his loyalty to the orchestra and to the music director and sworn to be true to the artistic vision that had brought the symphony to the brink of a recording contract. However, once this action had failed and the conductor who had championed him was no longer associated with the ensemble, he quickly changed his stripes. In all probability, he thought of himself as a possible, future music director in Pottstown. In fact, during the years of hiatus when the symphony had no music director but was represented in its reduced season by several guest conductors from the region, he did conduct one or two performances of Handel's *Messiah*. Thereafter, as the orchestra fell into opprobrium, he, too, disappeared from the scene.

Almost a month lapsed before there was much of an echo from the press. The local newspaper, The Mercury, which had seldom given the Pottstown Symphony any attention and had consciously ignored it for years as a factor in regional development, printed the following: "The symphony has been recognized as a gem in Pottstown, as few towns this size have the ability to maintain an orchestra. Much of the credit goes to the influence for years of the late Porter Eidam."[159] It was the local newspaper furthering the myth. About the recently departed music director who, in her six years at the helm of the orchestra had made all this possible, the newspaper said: "In recent years [the music director] has provided a spark as conductor, bringing her considerable talent and personality to performances."[160]

The Philadelphia Inquirer and its critic, David Patrick Stearns, came much closer to the truth in the headline which appeared in the "Enquirer" on 11 June 2008. It read, simply, "It sounds grim for Pottstown"[161]

---

[159] Pottstown Mercury 21 May 2008: "Resignations must not deter local symphony from moving forward".
[160] Ibid.
[161] "Philadelphia Inquirer". Issue of 11 June 2008.

Years later, it became evident to a growing circle of public and funders that the galloping misery present within the Pottstown Symphony Orchestra Association was not the fault of the music director and executive director but that of certain, key members of the board and that the roots of this problem could be traced back several decades. The former vice-president of the organization, the former drama teacher and now its newly elected president, wrote to the musicians in an open letter: "The Board of Directors of the Pottstown Symphony Orchestra Association has come to the difficult decision to postpone and/or cancel the remainder of the 2009-10 season. This decision is effective immediately...The PSOA is not threatened by bankruptcy and that is why we took this action to avoid the inability to pay, first and foremost, our highly valued musicians. Twenty-one months ago, the board of directors was left with a debt of $125,000+, a community that felt disenfranchised and unconnected to the PSO, and our orchestra members frustrated. The current management, in a short 21 months, has reduced the debt, re-engaged the community, and worked very closely with the orchestra committee to build a strong, transparent, and trusting relationship with our musicians."[162] The remaining, surviving but emaciated board of directors, had finally done that which had been recommended in 2007 by the former board member and head of the Philadelphia based audio firm and by the executive director in his white paper of February, 2008. They had cancelled the current season in an attempt to; finally, curb the financial blood-letting the symphony had been experiencing since 2001. (See chapter 5). It was only that this action was implemented at least three if not more years too late.

By December, 2010, the Pottstown Symphony's web presence had disappeared. At first, the then provider for the site, GoDaddy.com, had posted a notice at that URL requesting the owner of the site to contact them at a special number. This number was that of their credit and collection service.

The final holiday concert of the Pottstown Symphony (and possibly conclusively the final concert for the organization) was performed on 11 December 2010. A regional savings bank which had paid for this concert as a special holiday gift to its depositors and which distributed tickets only among its patrons had demanded that the concert be performed or they be repaid the $14,000 donation they had made the previous year. In 2009, this concert had been cancelled by a blizzard in the area. It was clear at this point

---

[162] Letter/Email from the then sitting President of the Pottstown Symphony Orchestra Association to the PSOA's performing musicians dated 26 January 2010.

that the repayment of the $14,000 to this bank was no longer an option for the Pottstown Symphony and its board.

In January, 2011, the banker who had betrayed the group of fellow board members seeking to reform the Pottstown Symphony revealed in a discussion with one of the members of that reform group how he "is really sorry for what he has done…[He] also realizes the damage this action has caused…to his community as a whole."[163]

Shortly thereafter, all links and other information taking one to a symphony presence on the web had disappeared. The aggressive and some believe also unstable board member who came from the Business on Board organization became the association's final president. At that stage, following or during a period where he was also acting executive director of the Pottstown Symphony, he was otherwise unemployed. The precise chronology of his curriculum vitae at this point is somewhat unclear. The former president, the wife of the headmaster, has departed from Pottstown as have several of the others in this story. The first board president, with the over 20 year tenure, was also dismissed from her position as superintendent of schools and assumed a job on the faculty of a private college in the area. Later, she also became part of an educational foundation in Pottstown.

The regional newspapers and the media make no mention any longer of the Pottstown Symphony, and rarely of the fact that an orchestra ever existed there, excepting an occasional lone-wolf plea that the symphony come back, someday. On 21 November 2011, there was an item appearing on an internet search engine[164] which listed a new management team for the orchestra. This team consisted of the first of the association's former presidents, the school superintendent described in this narrative, who was listed as chief operating officer and several attorneys, one of whom is the senior attorney and partner in the law office that employs the Pottstown Symphony's council and who, himself, was the initial "Mr. X" who was so active in 2005 and who abandoned the orchestra less than a year later.

The last of the PSOA's former presidents and the candidate who came to the symphony from the Business on Board program is listed on his LinkedIn.com web entry as "Academic Advisor and Adjunct Faculty" at a local community college.

It seems as if the Pottstown Symphony Orchestra is now nothing but a name.

---

[163] Memo from former Executive Director of the Pottstown Symphony to Attorney Nancy Abrams dated 11 January 2011.
[164] http://companies.lead411.com/company_PottstownSymphonyOrchestra.com.

The *United States Internal Revenue Service* has informed this author on 16 July 2012 that the non-profit status enjoyed by the Pottstown Symphony Orchestra Association was revoked by the IRS in July, 2012.[165]

As an active, recognized, tax-exempt and cultural entity contributing to life in its community and in the greater region, this organization has now ceased to exist.

---

[165] Telephone conversation with IRS employee based at its offices in Cincinnati, OH, ID 100704574, on 16 July 2012.

9. CONCLUSIONS

At the conclusion of this narrative, the one question which remains is how, if at all, this outcome could have been prevented. The dysfunctional nature of the Pottstown Symphony and its board had very deep roots. If you will recall, in an earlier chapter when mentioning the then conductor Kenneth Morse and the status of his fledgling ensemble, there were newspaper references to difficulties which, even then, endangered the very existence of the orchestra. As time progressed and the educational focus of William Lamb was replaced by the more professional impetus brought to the organization by Porter Eidam, the symphony changed in its outward, but not in its inward ability to critically evaluate itself. Over many years, it was consistently the music director in Pottstown who also delivered the drive towards progress and towards an orchestra which would take on more importance than that of being simply a community organization.

Perhaps this, in fact, was the initial problem. It is clear that the various music directors the Pottstown Symphony has engaged in its long history were also ambitious persons with an eye to what the symphony could also have done for their careers. There is nothing negative in this statement. It is something we all expect from a position, that it become a possible stepping-stone to something bigger and better. The problem in Pottstown is that this impetus should have come, first and foremost, from the board and not from the artistic side. Had the drive to become bigger and better also been matched by a comparable support from the board and business leaders within the greater Pottstown community, there would have also developed within the orchestra a sense of motivation and belonging. However, in the entire narrative of this long and sad history, one factor remains paramount. That factor is the disconnection which always existed between the ambitions of the artistic leadership and the need of the board to "belong" to the community. These two elements cannot be reconciled, especially in an environment where the unprofessionalism of most of the board, its inexperience with normal and effective business models which govern non-profits and cultural institutions, and its passive acknowledgement but not acceptance of its fiduciary role led to over 20 years of stagnation.

There were many opportunities to change this situation and introduce new patterns of behavior that would have been adequate to reverse the tide driving the symphony into ruin. An early decision by the board to forbid the dual membership of any individual as board member and musician in the orchestra [except in cases of non-voting, employee associate directors such as the music director, personnel contractors or executive director] would have, much later, helped to eliminate the problem of board loyalty. We have seen in the matter with the American Federation of Musicians and the betrayal of board confidences to the labor union and its representatives, how such a rule, strictly enforced, could have helped to protect the organization's internal confidences and strengthened its position in fending off the threats of union bullying.

The establishment of fiscal policies with prudent and accurate budgets and an effective business plan would have clearly delineated the trend, evident as early as 2002, that the symphony was entering a downward spiral. The elimination of such line items as marketing costs from the budget and, instead, the insertion of simply an entry for "printing" as was the case with the 2004 budget projections, gave many on the board the impression that certain "things" happen by themselves. This contributed to the all-volunteer mentality that had established itself in Pottstown and denied the need to provide adequate resources for the organization's activities. The continuation of this mentality then led to an abrogation of the need to fundraise and, eventually, the transfer of this obligation entirely onto the shoulders of the symphony's second executive director with the board doing nothing more than sitting back and repeatedly asking the question: "where's the beef?"

The role of the chief executive was also never fully addressed. On the one hand this board was willing to give a title to anyone who could walk and breathe but the transfer of authority to this person was quite another matter. This was a board of school teachers used to dealing with children and not of educated adults who had more than rudimentary experience in the wider business world. This board regularly assigned tasks to its management team consisting of the music director and executive director without the moral or financial support or authority to properly and effectively make and implement decisions. The issue at stake was always one of power and of board authority. It seemed to be the policy of the board that the finding of a scapegoat should a project fail was its main priority instead of supplying resources, authority and support to prevent this failure. The attitude faced by the executive staff and those outside the board's inner circle in their eternal pleas for financial support and board engagement in the management of the orchestra, finds an echo in the words of the innkeeper, Gardena to the Surveyor K. in Kafka's novel, *The Castle*: "You are not from the castle, you are not from the village, you are nothing."[166]

Often decisions made by the board of the Pottstown Symphony simply received no vote. There was often no protocol and no documentation of any

---

[166] Franz Kafka: *Das Schloss:* "Sie sind nicht aus dem Schloss, Sie sind nicht aus dem Dorfe, Sie sind nichts."

kind to prove or disprove that the board had agreed to anything. This was many times the case with the selection and approval of the coming concert season, a decision always made in January or February, as well as with other activities initiated in the name of and for the good of the ensemble. It was often the case that a project would be approved and the board would volunteer for the project, distributing advertising and, sometimes, delivering pleas for public support, but would eventually deny it had ever done so. This was the case with the board in 2007 when it tacitly approved a fund-raising, benefit concert, for the Pottstown Symphony to be held in June 2008 featuring the appearance of a big band in the region, created posters and flyers for the event, signed the check for the deposit to secure the big band, presented the event at several of its mini-fundraising activities and in the lobby of the Hill School before and after concerts and, at the end, cancelled the event claiming it had never given its approval to the concept. This was a board ever seeking a reason to deny it had ever assumed the authority and responsibility for its actions.

This board had also lost its link with the community. Its dramatic debt picture, its history of late payments or, in many cases, no payment, soured the attitudes of the merchants in Pottstown and the vicinity against the symphony and its board. In several cases, this board had tried to push the responsibility for its actions onto others. The issue with the printing company outside of Pottstown which was left with unpaid bills totaling more than $10,000 was one where the former treasurer of the board, in negotiating a deal for a venue for the spring pops concert in that year, had inadequately secured the venue and the agreement with the printer to use his property for that event was never codified in a contract. The verbal deal was simple. The symphony would use the land behind the printing plant to set up a large tent to house the orchestra and guests and the printing company would be allowed to invite a number of its best customers. In exchange for these invitations, the orchestra would pay the costs but the printing company would guarantee the symphony its printing, for one season, for free. It was that easy but, without a contract, the misunderstandings grew and led to the symphony facing significant outstanding costs and being threatened with legal ramifications were it not to reconcile these invoices.

The same policies held sway in the relationship of the Pottstown Symphony with Emmanuel Lutheran Church and its agreement with the congregation to share the profits of the chamber music concerts. Up until December, 2006, this relationship went well and was conducted professionally. After January 2007, however, the officers at the symphony simply "forgot" to pay the church which led to a collapse of the relationship between the church and the orchestra and its board which was never quite repaired. Remember, as has been related in an earlier chapter, the former pastor of the church advised the symphony and its officers, following the departure of the music director and executive director, that he was no longer interested in allowing the Pottstown Symphony to use Emmanuel as a concert venue. His message was, clearly, that with the persons he could trust having left the scene; he was not willing to again assume the significant risks associated with a further and future partnership with the symphony's board.

The symphony board also failed in its inability to structure its planning and to set a responsible program for fundraising and administrative development from year to year that was in sync with its stated long-range strategic planning goals. In its inability to do so, it also failed to set sound policies for the operation of the organization.

Of course, the internal political squabbles in the association and the evolution of the board into the "full board" and the, parallel "rogue board" which made its decisions in the parking lot following the general meetings, did nothing to foster the development of the organization into, as they would later call themselves in the symphony's "Mission Statement", "the premiere arts and cultural center in the Pottstown region".[167]

Above all, however, the reason for the failure of this organization was its fundamentally dysfunctional makeup, both at a personal and at an organizational level. Critical points made by Dr. Albert J. Bernstein in his 2009 book, *Am I the only Sane One Working Here? 101 Solutions for Surviving Office Insanity*,[168] are uniquely pertinent to the situation which existed in the board of the Pottstown Symphony. Bernstein cites a number of danger signs in a presumably diseased organization, among them being the copious posting of vision or value statements rife with vague sounding appellations such as "excellence" and/or "quality", the general attitude among management that an employee who wishes to address a problem is suffering from some sort of personality disorder and is a problem in himself, the insistence that the only solution to problems is to be found via motivational seminars such as board retreats, the regular editing of the organization's history to seem to make executive decisions more important than they genuinely were, the discouraging of any written commitments, the communication of directions in a vague and often marginally threatening manner, the rewarding of internal competition as opposed to internal teamwork, and the placement of any decision-making power at the highest level within the organization and only at that level and the inability to delegate coupled with the understanding of delegation as meaning the

---

[167] PSOA Strategic Planning Committee "Vision Statement" from 20 February 2008.
[168] http://jobs.aol.com/articlesIprintarticle/2009/11/06/workplace-is-dysfunctional/?

person to whom the task has been assigned is also not given the powers needed to perform it. This delegation and decision making issue reached such a degree of absurdity in the Pottstown Symphony that the decision as to which candidate would be named to a newly created, part-time position of administrative assistant was all but taken away from the executive director to whom this person was to report. The board president of 20 years tenure had demanded that she be the only one qualified to make such an "important" personnel decision. Only through repeated protests and insistence that it must be done differently, that the line supervisor was also entitled to make the hiring decision and that the board president had no role to play in this decision once the position itself, the job description and the funding therefore were in place and approved, did the executive director win on this point. On top of all these factors, however, Dr. Bernstein also cites several more which were part of the cancer that eventually consumed the Pottstown Symphony. He mentions the tight control of resources [in his first term as executive director (2005-2006) access to the financial records of the association was denied to the executive director and the Association's books were kept at an outside location], the regularly repeated message to the management team that it could consider itself lucky to have a job and that job could be easily lost, and the enforcement of rules based upon who one was rather than what one does. This latter, double standard was clearly evident in the decision of the board executives and their executive and governance committees to impeach a critical board member but to protect one who consciously and with clearly destructive or self-serving intentions had betrayed the organization on many instances to the labor union. Also, the former president of the board who, most probably, initiated the action which cost the symphony several of its desperately needed educational concerts, had been appointed an honorary board member even though in her 20 or more years of service she had systematically driven the organization into financial ruin through mismanagement, pettiness and her inability to understand both her role and that of the organization in the development of Pottstown as a community.

In these pages, I have tried to present what many of you may deem to be a horror tale which, in its entirety, could not have happened. Some of you may think that portions of this narrative have been invented or that there have been exaggerations of fact or embellishments to emphasize the seriousness of the occurrences narrated here. It would have been my fondest wish to be able to comfort you with the assurances that, indeed, this was so. However, this story is not a fantasy. It is not a product of my over-active imagination just as it is not intended to frighten anyone interested in pursuing a career in orchestra management from doing so. The real purpose of this book is to alert you to some of the danger signs which could lead to situations where your livelihoods and those of your loved-ones are put in jeopardy by organizations which, by their simply dysfunctional nature, have little or no interest in the progress made by their organization but are only concerned with their own sense of self-importance.

There have been other works written which document, from a financial and often legal view, the reasons for the decline of a cultural organization. Some of them have been mentioned here, most notably the book by Dr. Thomas Wolf and Nancy Glaze: *And the Band Stopped Playing*.[169] However, Dr. Wolf and Ms. Glaze, in their excellent analysis, are also evaluating the reasons for the decline and fall of an orchestra, the San José Symphony in California, which had achieved a great degree of professionalism and had been in existence for 125 years at the point it closed its doors forever. The Pottstown Symphony had, at the time of its closing and for the years leading up to its ultimate end, slavishly resisted any drive to engage the organization and its board in any sort of professional behavior. Marketing and other initiatives, developed by others outside the board or by the association's employees, never received any real degree of support. The attitude towards the employees and their ideas was quite simple. If one ignored them, they would go away and the useless board member retreats the headmaster's wife had organized dedicated valuable hours which could have been spent in problem solving to the folding of paper airplanes and the construction of bridges with building blocks. The final employees of this organization refused to "go away" until it became clear that by further playing at this charade they would be hurting themselves more than any benefit they could bring to the organization. At that point, in the spring of 2008, there was nothing more than a skeleton. The adopted self-importance of the board showed itself to remarkably resemble the tale of the "Emperor's New Clothes". With the departure of the last hint of genuine professional experience from the industry side and the loss of its active board members, of the support of Emmanuel Lutheran and of its season sponsor and others, it stood there as naked as on the day it had been born. To its shame, however, it never noticed this nakedness.

The news that the Internal Revenue Service had revoked the non-profit status of the Pottstown Symphony was the final stroke. There is no orchestra any longer except, perhaps, in a legal sense. The Pottstown Symphony Orchestra Association is unable to dissolve itself or seek bankruptcy protection as long as it still faces litigation. No one will donate to an

---

[169] Dr. Thomas Wolf & Nancy Glaze: *And the Band stopped Playing – The Rise and Fall of the San José Symphony.* (Wolf, Keens & Company, Cambridge, MA 2005).

organization knowing that their donation no longer brings with it any tax advantage. The constant drafting and re-drafting of by-laws, governance documents, impeachment documents, and other, senseless administrative rituals, were nothing more than a guise to avoid the real work of this orchestra and of its board, i.e. providing the support and resources necessary to achieve the goal it set of becoming a regional ensemble.

In the final four years of its existence, the Pottstown Symphony was continually on life support. Its death was painful to watch and it was slow. However, that it would come was never in doubt. The signs of its dry-rot were too prevalent and the decay too well established for the ultimate fate of the organization to have had anything but an unhappy outcome. It is unclear what actually happened in the last two or three years the symphony still existed. At the end, there was, simply, no more music. The departed executive director had, in late-2007, developed a low-budget, emergency fund-raising campaign together with the art director and then board member. It was a risky enterprise that one only ventured upon once and in times of most dire need. It depicted an empty theatre with an empty orchestra set-up on the stage and with the headline: "Without you, there will be no Music". At the end, the public left, the musicians lost their trust in the ensemble, in themselves, and in many of their colleagues and the music stopped.

In this history of the last years of this ensemble we also find parallels to the social struggle ripping apart the world in the form of the present economic crisis. The international recession, bankruptcy of nations and massive unemployment and world hunger must be seen against the backdrop of a super-rich and privileged minority. A recent and shocking statistic was published by the Wall Street Journal in its issue of 22 July 2012. That statistic reveals that close to $32 trillion is being hidden from tax authorities around the world in offshore accounts. "That wealth means that the problem of inequality in wealth and income is actually worse than suspected"[170] In real terms, this amount has been estimated as being equal to $5,000 for every man, woman and child on the planet[171]. In the context of this story, where repeatedly references have been made to the prevalent and elitist worth in which the board of the Pottstown Symphony had held itself, this asocial behavior of many of the wealthiest in our society is mirrored in the behavior of the board in Pottstown. Remember the phrase uttered by the second

---

[170] McKinnon, John D.: Tax Justice Network: "Wealth Held in Tax Havens Skyrockets". Printed in The Wall Street Journal from 22 July 2012.
[171] United States Census Bureau – World POPClock Projections. July 2012 – July 2013 report a world population of 7.117 billion persons.

board president: "well, she's going blind anyway" or the elitist pronouncement by the insurance company partner and board member that the board is infallible and the employees are simply to behave. In Pottstown, this was a return to the middle ages, to a mentality where the nobility held its serfs in bondage and reacted at will, responding only to its interests and to its selfish need to control wealth and to remain in power. I look upon this story with the Pottstown Symphony as a mini drama reflecting the combat between social and asocial forces in our society. In Pottstown, no one won this battle. The community lost its orchestra and much of its surviving dignity, the board lost in power and influence and was forced to swallow the disgrace of its own and self-initiated degradation and the employees lost their positions and, in part, a segment of their futures. This is what may also happen as the ongoing socio-economic war continues. We have placed personal gain above the common good much as had the members of the board of the Pottstown Symphony.

In writing this book I have arrived at a uniquely personal conclusion, one that seems, superficially, asocial and anti-art but which, perhaps, presents a mechanism which could prevent what happened here from repeating itself with other organizations of similar makeup. After 40 years in the music business, in all facets of its enterprise, I have reached the simple conclusion that there are either too many arts organizations in the United States, many of them operating at amateur level or below and some showing a similar symptomatic decay as did the Pottstown Symphony, or that the criteria for the establishment of such a tax exempt organization and its continued recognition as such are, simply, much too lax. Cultural organizations in the USA each hold an Internal Revenue Service awarded 501(c) 3 or non-profit status and each is tax-exempt. All of these organizations exist, more or less, from public trust and public money. In the granting of this tax-exempt status, I see an intrinsic authority given to the Internal Revenue Service and other, state and local governing bodies, allowing them much more stringently and in finer detail to put each and every such organization under an infinitely stronger microscope – examining not only its tax returns but also its personnel policies, its governance and the makeup and professional qualifications of its board of directors. It took a major, global recession to nudge the Pottstown Symphony Orchestra Association over the precipice at which it was standing for almost 20 years, all the time the public and funders were being duped by the simple designation, "tax-exempt non-profit". Better governmental oversight could have prevented this deception, perhaps even a decade earlier, and kept the agony and human misery in this narrative from ever happening.

As you drive through the borough of Pottstown, you are immediately impressed by the timing of the town's traffic lights and by their positioning in a way that forces the traveler to closely observe the community in all its decay and all its misery. They compel the visitor to count the abandoned buildings and take under scrutiny the numbers of homeless and the filth on the streets. You are impressed by the lack of activity in this town, by the sluggish movement of its people and the disinterest they seem to take in their own village. The timing of these lights delays your speedy trip through the Pottstown borough by several unending minutes. They give you a chance to reflect on the fate of this community, perhaps in pity and, perhaps also in disgust. The traffic semaphores in Pottstown serve as a sentinel, warning of this internal and external decay and as a reminder of the gap that exists between those who "have" and those who dare no longer hope to "have."

In conclusion, there are many poets who have dedicated lines to the description of the sorts of injustices that are described in this book. One of these is Wilhelm Mueller who, in his "Leiermann"[172], tells of the poor musician who "barefoot on the ice sways before his empty plate", of the man who "no one will hear and who no one watches". The growling of the hounds and the cold and the masses ignoring his plight cannot bring him from turning his melodies on his hurdy-gurdy and are a further symbol of the hostility and inhuman contempt we encounter, ever-present in our modern society. Mueller asks the question of us whether we will go with this old man. The hurdy-gurdy man is a metaphor for the state of humanity, for the state of the arts today and for the general superficiality and loss of worth that have entered our culture. We have become so overwhelmed by corruption and lies that we defend ourselves by looking beyond that which puts us most in peril. We have become numb to the assaults on our sensibilities and on our existence. Crying and alone in the wilderness of cities, the singer asks in this poem if "you will turn also my songs on your hurdy-gurdy?" His is the voice of the few, pleading in the name of the lost values of the many.

It is we, the givers of art and culture, who have become the "hurdy-gurdy" players of our time, grinding out our melodies at the whim and for the pleasure of many for whom this beauty means nothing. It is in our hands to

---

[172] Wilhelm Mueller (1794 – 1827): "Der Leiermann": Drüben hinter'm Dorfe, Steht ein Leiermann, Und mit starren Fingern, Dreht er was er kann. Barfuß auf dem Eise, Wankt er hin und her; Und sein kleiner Teller, Bleibt ihm immer leer. Keiner mag ihn hören, Keiner sieht ihn an; Und die Hunde knurren um den alten Mann. Und er läßt es gehen, Alles, wie es will. Dreht, und seine Leier steht ihm nimmer still. Wunderlicher Alter, Soll ich mit dir gehen? Willst zu meinen Liedern Deine Leier drehn?"

change this, to make of this new century one where the power of artistic expression and the ethics of a critical and vocal culture would decisively influence our ability to assess and to change the world around us. This is as true in the arts as it is in politics and in our business lives. It impacts all facets of our existence and that of our children and of their children to come. What had happened at this time and in this place, in Pottstown many years ago, is symptomatic of the artistic and cultural devolution that has scarred the final decades of the 20th century. These events that took place in Pottstown would not have taken place had that same sense of cultural and ethical worth been present in this community and on this board of directors at this critical time in the development of this orchestra. That this organization could continue for so long as it had and, at the end, simply disappear from the landscape, unlamented by the region which it had served and could have further served for many years to come, is symptomatic of the dearth of understanding of the role and influence the arts can play in the creation and the maintenance of an ethical society.

We can now make a beginning and we can alter this downward spiral and give back to ourselves and to our hurdy-gurdy man the dignity that was once his and, with that dignity, restore this selfsame ethical balance to our culture and to ourselves. I ask you to look upon this narrative as a pathfinder, as a messenger urging us to restore that worth to its rightful place in the continuum of a greater society and not, as T.S. Eliot so sadly commented, to watch the edifice of human integrity be further weakened as it was, in Pottstown, in those final days.

"This is the way the world ends

Not with a bang but a whimper."[173]

---

[173] T.S. Eliot: "The Hollow Men". *The Hollow Men* Parts I, II, and IV in *Poems: 1909–1925*. Dial, 1925.

10. ACKNOWLEDGMENTS

I would like to express my special thanks to several former board members and former employees of the Pottstown Symphony Orchestra Association who have kindly assisted me in confirming the accuracy of this book and of the facts therein. Among these are Dr. William Nash and Mr. Michael Purdy in addition to several others who have been associated with the Pottstown Symphony Orchestra Association and its board but who, for personal reasons, wish to remain anonymous. Their support and counsel has been invaluable in making this narrative as complete and accurate as possible.

I wish to express my special gratitude to Mr. Colin Attwell of Claudio Records in the UK for his support, his advice and his belief in the message contained in this book. His selfless offer to assume the time and costs to record the audio version of this volume and his invaluable assistance with other aspects of this presentation are something I will never forget and for which I remain eternally grateful.

I would also like to express my gratitude to Dr. Maria Thompson Corley who donated many hours to critical review of these contents and made many suggestions all of which went into improving this manuscript.

Similarly, I wish to thank Mr. Lutz Kirchhof, internationally known and respected lutenist and expert in the recording and music industry, for his help in making this work as professional and accurate as possible.

My gratitude also goes out to Prof. Dr. Steven Paul for his insights into the problems described in this volume, his careful examination of the arguments therein and the unselfish contribution of his immense wealth of knowledge and experience gained in almost 50 years as a music industry professional, Grammy winning producer and educator.

Finally, I wish to thank Christel Döllstädt who selflessly tolerated my long hours and many months of self-induced isolation that went into writing this work and who significantly contributed to the extensive discussions that went into the planning and realization of this book.

Sponsors of this project

Through their generous sponsorship, the following persons have made possible the publication of THE BOARD. I wish to express my sincere thanks to them for their engagement for this project and for helping to make this story known to others for whom it has been written and who, it is hoped, will profit from the lessons this history has to teach.

Georg and Ingeborg Obermeyer - Germany

Prof. Ab Koster and Hendrika Koster – The Netherlands

There are also a number of donors who have given generously to help make this book a reality but, for personal reasons, wish to remain anonymous. This list is international in scope and includes supporters and influential colleagues in the entertainment industry from Costa Rica, Germany, The Czech Republic, Australia, the USA and Canada.

My thanks go out to these persons as well as my acknowledgement of them in this form and according to their wishes.

NOTE: Subsequent to the completion of this book, one outstanding matter of litigation against the Pottstown Symphony Orchestra Association was, reluctantly and unsatisfactorily, laid to rest. The delaying tactics of the PSOA's attorney coupled with his litany of excuses as to why the action could not progress and the opposing attorney's failure to address issues of Statute of Limitations in a timely and effective fashion, have brought this matter to a state of perpetual stagnation with no hope of any justifiable settlement. Whether there is additional litigation pending against the Pottstown Symphony Orchestra Association at this time is unknown to this author.

www.ingramcontent.com/pod-product-compliance
Lightning Source LLC
Chambersburg PA
CBHW020423220526
45464CB00002B/538